A Note From Rick Renner

I am on a personal quest to see a "revival of the Bible" so people can establish their lives on a firm foundation that will stand strong and endure the test when the end-time storm winds begin to intensify.

In order to experience a revival of the Bible in your personal life, it is important to take time each day to read, receive, and apply its truths to your life. James tells us that if we will continue in the perfect law of liberty — refusing to be forgetful hearers but determined to be doers — we will be blessed in our ways. As you watch or listen to the programs in this series and work through this corresponding study guide, I trust that you will search the Scriptures and allow the Holy Spirit to help you hear something new from God's Word that applies specifically to your life. I encourage you to be a doer of the Word that He reveals to you. Whatever the cost, I assure you — it will be worth it.

> Thy words were found, and I did eat them;
> and thy word was unto me the joy and rejoicing of mine heart:
> for I am called by thy name, O Lord God of hosts.
> — Jeremiah 15:16

Your brother and friend in Jesus Christ,

Rick Renner

Understanding Fivefold Ministry

Copyright © 2019 by Rick Renner
8316 E. 73rd St.
Tulsa, Oklahoma 74133

Published by Rick Renner Ministries
www.renner.org

ISBN 13: 978-1-68031-621-6

eBook ISBN 13: 978-1-68031-659-9

How To Use This Study Guide

This ten-lesson study guide corresponds to *"Understanding Fivefold Ministry" With Rick Renner* (Renner TV). Each lesson in this study guide covers a topic that is addressed during the program series, with questions and references supplied to draw you deeper into your own private study of the Scriptures on this subject.

To derive the most benefit from this study guide, consider the following:

First, watch or listen to the program prior to working through the corresponding lesson in this guide. (Programs can also be viewed at **renner.org** by clicking on the Media/Archives links.)

Second, take the time to look up the scriptures included in each lesson. Prayerfully consider their application to your own life.

Third, use a journal or notebook to make note of your answers to each lesson's Study Questions and Practical Application challenges.

Fourth, invest specific time in prayer and in the Word of God to consult with the Holy Spirit. Write down the scriptures or insights He reveals to you about being filled with the Spirit and empowered by Him in your daily life.

Finally, take action! Whatever the Lord tells you to do according to His Word, do it.

For added insights on this subject, it is recommended that you obtain Rick Renner's book *Chosen By God: Stepping Into the Abundant Life That God Fashioned for You.* You may also select from Rick's other available resources by placing your order at **renner.org** or by calling 1-800-742-5593.

TOPIC

The Ministry of the Apostle, Part 1

SCRIPTURES

1. **Ephesians 4:11** — And he gave some, apostles; and some, prophets; and some, evangelists; and some, pastors and teachers.

GREEK WORDS

1. "apostle" — ἀπόστολος (*apostolos*): a compound of ἀπό (*apo*) and στέλλω (*stello*); the word ἀπό (*apo*) means away, and the word στέλλω (*stello*) means "I send"; compounded, they form the word *apostolos*, which means one who is sent away; pictures a messenger, an envoy, or a delegate; one commissioned by another to represent him in some way; in the New Testament, it depicts a minister sent by Jesus Christ or by the Church; an apostle. The word στέλλω (*stello*) — the second part of the word "apostle" — is derived from στολος (*stolos*), which depicts a military expedition, a campaign, a tour, armed forces, army, navy, or a military entourage

SYNOPSIS

The ten lessons in this study on *Understanding Fivefold Ministry* will focus on the following topics:

- The Ministry of the *Apostle*
- The Ministry of the *Prophet*
- The Ministry of the *Evangelist*
- The Ministry of the *Pastor*
- The Ministry of the *Teacher*

The emphasis of this lesson:

Apostles are the first of the fivefold ministry gifts Jesus gave to the Church. They are uniquely called and equipped to be on the front-

lines of ministry, taking new ground and establishing God's Kingdom throughout the world.

The Mount of Olives is quite a magnificent site near the city of Jerusalem. It was a favorite place Jesus frequented — a place where He regularly met and prayed with His apostles. It was the place where He charged them with the Great Commission, the place from where He ascended into Heaven, and the place where He promised them the precious gift of the Holy Spirit. As apostles, they were supernaturally empowered to be Jesus' witnesses, performing signs and wonders and evangelizing the lost.

When Jesus finished His work on the earth, He birthed His Church to continue what He started. To help in every aspect of this endeavor, He gave the Church what is called the fivefold ministry gifts. The apostle Paul describes these gifts in Ephesians 4:11. "And he gave some, apostles; and some, prophets; and some, evangelists; and some, pastors and teachers." The truth is, there is much confusion regarding these very important New Testament terms, especially on the topic of apostles.

You've probably heard about the *apostles* and read about them, but who were they? What were they called to do? Are there still apostles in the world today, and if so, who are they and what do they do? Let's take a look at what the Bible says about apostles and gain the historical perspective on the origin and meaning of this word.

There Are Misconceptions About Apostles

Whether you have grown up in church or got saved at a later time in life, there are many ideas and teachings regarding apostles that are simply not true. For instance, there are certain mainline denominations that believe and teach things like:

- Apostles and prophets don't exist in today's world.
- The role of apostles and prophets passed away with the end of the apostolic age.
- There were only 12 apostles, and that was it.
- It is arrogant for anyone to say he or she is an apostle.
- "Missionaries" are the closest thing to an apostle in today's world.

None of these things are true.

Neither is it correct to label nearly everyone in ministry as an apostle, which is what some charismatic denominations claim. For example, if a person is gifted with strong faith, they are called an "apostle of faith." If they are very wise in the area of finances, they are called and "apostle of finances." Likewise, if someone is anointed in the area of worship, he or she is called an "apostle of worship." However, there are no such things as any of these.

Although a person can be highly gifted and anointed in a certain area — such as worship, faith, and finances — they are not apostles. They are leaders and pioneers operating on the cutting edge of these areas of ministry. We can and should appreciate the anointing on their lives, but to call them apostles is to misuse the word and dilute the weight of its true meaning.

What Is an 'Apostle'?

It is important to note that the word "apostle" was not a term that originated from Scripture. It was a secular term that had very clear meanings. If you were a person living in New Testament times and you heard the word "apostle," the definition and the imagery of the word would have been very different than what our ears hear nearly 2,000 years later.

The word "apostle" is the Greek word *apostolos*. It is a compound of the word *apo*, which means *away*, and the word *stello*, which means *I send*. When you compound these two words together, it forms the word *apostolos*; meaning *one who is sent away, a messenger, an envoy* or *a delegate*. It is *one commissioned by another to represent him in some way*. In the New Testament, *it depicts a minister sent by Jesus Christ or by the Church*, and it is translated as the word "apostle."

Going a little deeper, the word *stello* — the second part of the word *apostolos* — is derived from the word *stolos*, which depicts *a military expedition, campaign, or tour*; it pictures *armed forces, such as an army, a navy, or a military entourage*. This lets us know that apostolic ministry is frontline ministry. Like a military expedition that ventures into new territory to crush the enemy, apostles are highly trained individuals that are sent with the power of God to crush the enemy and to take new territory for the Kingdom of God.

What is interesting is that the word *apostolos* appears 79 times in the New Testament. The root of *apostolos* — the word *apostello* — appears no less than 131 times in the New Testament and more than 700 times in the Greek Septuagint. When a word is used this frequently, its meaning is very well established in Scripture.

At first glance, it may seem that the definition of this word *apostolos* — *one who is sent away* — denoted one who had been dismissed, set aside, or rejected. But this word didn't refer to a person sent away in dishonor or disgrace. On the contrary, the word *apostolos* is a term of great honor that referred to a person who was personally selected, commissioned, and sent on an assignment on behalf of a very powerful government or individual. This person wasn't merely sent off; he was empowered, invested with authority, and then dispatched to accomplish a special task.

What Did New Testament Ears Hear When They Heard the Word 'Apostle'?

Taking into account the root meaning of the word "apostle," there were four distinct images and understandings that came to the minds of the New Testament hearers when they heard the word.

#1: The Admiral of a Fleet of Ships

During the time of the ancient Greek orator Demosthenes (384-322 BC), the word *apostolos* — from where we get the word "apostle" — was a naval term that described an admiral of a fleet of ships. The fleet of ships that traveled with him carried a specialized crew who accompanied and assisted the admiral. Thus, the admiral never traveled alone; he always had a crew with him.

As they were sent out to sea, their mission was to locate territories where civilization was non-existent. Once an uncivilized region was identified, the admiral — along with his specialized, apostolic crew and all their cargo and belongings — would disembark the ship, settle down, and work as a team to establish a new community in the new region.

As soon as the admiral (the *apostolos*) made it to the mainland, he became the architect of the new colony, giving oversight for the construction of the new society. He remained the top leader and gave the orders on what to do. With his team, they would begin the process of transforming a strange land into a replica of life as they believed it should be. Their purpose was the total colonization of the new territory — to recreate their culture and language in a new place.

Within this special fleet of ships were the personnel and cargo required to replicate a new culture, a new life, and a new community. When that fleet pulled up to shore, it contained every specialized worker needed to train people, to build roads, to construct buildings, and to teach uncivilized natives how to read, write, and function in a new kind of society.

Once the job was complete and the area was colonized, the admiral and many of the team members got back onto the ships and launched out to sea again to find another uncivilized area to repeat the colonization process all over again in another new location.

Think how this applies to the work of an apostle...

He was a team leader, the architect of a new church, who worked alongside others, to build the Church in new places. This frontline leader took his team and replicated the life of the Church of Jesus Christ everywhere they went. The specialized workers with him taught people how to know and speak the truth of God's Word. Once the Church was established, the apostle would pack up certain members of his team and travel to another area where the Gospel was unknown and begin the process all over again.

#2: A Passport That Guaranteed the Right of Passage

The word *apostolos* — from where we get the word "apostle" — was so closely associated with the idea of traveling that it eventually became synonymous with the idea of *a passport* or a travel document. If a person wanted to leave a country, he had to possess a travel document that was essentially an exit visa, or a passport. This legal document was called an *apostolos* — the same word translated "apostle." This document guaranteed a person the right of passage and the ability to move freely from one place to another and enter territories where they had never been.

Think how this applies to the work of an apostle...

When the word *apostolos* was applied to New Testament individuals, it referred to apostles who were able to spiritually lead believers and churches in a journey they could never go on by themselves. The apostle would lead them to depths of revelation harder to attain without apostolic ministry. In this sense, an apostle was a *spiritual passport* that enabled believers and churches to journey into deep spiritual truths.

#3: A Personal Representative, an Ambassador

The word "apostle" — from the Greek word *apostolos* — was used to describe a person who had the authority to act in the stead of the one who sent him. For this reason, it was also used to depict an ambassador who represents his government.

This classical and secular meaning of the word *apostolos* was an envoy sent to do business on behalf of the one who sent him. Such people served as personal representatives, emissaries, messengers, diplomats, or ambassadors. They possessed clout and influence to speak and to act on behalf of the one who sent him on his assignment.

So when the *apostolos* spoke, his words were counted as the words of his sender. When the *apostolos* acted, his actions were interpreted as those of his sender. The connection between the sender and the person who was sent was virtually inseparable.

Think about how this applies to the work of an apostle...

An early New Testament "apostle" was the ambassador of Jesus Christ who was gifted with the spiritual clout and authority to speak and act on behalf of Christ — or on behalf of His Church. When he spoke, he spoke the words of Jesus. Likewise, when he acted, he acted on behalf of Jesus. The connection between the apostle and Christ Himself was inseparable.

#4: A Spiritual Leader

The fourth understanding that came to the minds of the New Testament hearers when they heard the word *apostolos* was quite unique. In classical times, the word *apostolos* also signified a person who was gifted by the gods and sent to the people as the gods' special messenger. The pagan population stood in awe of such individuals because they possessed supernatural knowledge and insight that was unavailable to the average man. This person was able to take people to new heights and depths spiritually that he or she could probably never reach on their own.

So even before the development of New Testament terminology, the word *apostolos* came to portray a spiritual leader whose insights would take people from one realm to the next.

Think how this applies to the work of an apostle...

A New Testament apostle was a spiritual leader enriched with supernatural insights. He had the ability to take people to places spiritually that they could probably never go to on their own. The insights and revelation the apostle had were not naturally obtained. This agrees with what the apostle Paul wrote in Galatians 1:11,12 — the Gospel he preached was not from a man but from the mouth of Jesus Himself.

So to New Testament Believers, the Word 'Apostle' Meant...

An apostle was **a spiritual admiral**, a spiritual architect, an overseer, a coordinator, and the chief leader responsible for "colonizing" new territories with the Word of God and with the culture of the New Testament Church.

An apostle was like **a spiritual passport**, providing passage from one spiritual dimension to another and his anointing would enable a church to journey into levels of spiritual growth that it would possibly never reach apart from the apostle's anointing.

An apostle was like **a spiritual ambassador** authorized to speak and to act on the Lord's behalf. He represented Jesus Christ and had the backing of God's Kingdom behind him, and as the emissary of Christ, he had the anointing and spiritual backing — the clout and authority — to get things accomplished.

Finally, an apostle was **a spiritual leader** that possessed supernatural insights given to him by Christ that were vital for the growth and the building up of the Church. Indeed, an apostle was specially selected, specially commissioned, and specially sent to represent the Lord in a variety of ways.

In our next lesson, we will discover that in addition to the 12 foundational apostles selected by Jesus during His ministry, there are many more apostles mentioned in the Bible.

STUDY QUESTIONS

Study to shew thyself approved unto God, a workman that needeth not to be ashamed, rightly dividing the word of truth.
— 2 Timothy 2:15

1. Prior to this lesson, what was your understanding of an apostle? Were you believing any misconceptions of what an apostle was? If so, what did you believe?

2. What new insights have you gained from this teaching about apostles? What were the names of these 12 men hand-picked by Jesus to be foundational apostles (*see* Mark 3:13-19; Luke 6:12-16)?

3. Of the 12 foundational apostles, who do you admire and who are you drawn to most? Why?

PRACTICAL APPLICATION

But be ye doers of the word, and not hearers only,
deceiving your own selves.
—James 1:22

1. In light of the historical and Scriptural meaning of the word "apostle" (*apostolos*) presented in this lesson, how have you seen this word misused or abused?

2. Who do you know of that is actually serving in the frontline ministry of apostle but without the title? In what specific ways are they carrying out the work of an apostle?

LESSON 2

TOPIC

The Ministry of the Apostle, Part 2

SCRIPTURES

1. **Ephesians 4:11** — And he gave some, apostles; and some, prophets; and some, evangelists; and some, pastors and teachers.

2. **1 Corinthians 9:1** — Am I not an apostle? am I not free? have I not seen Jesus Christ our Lord? are not ye my work in the Lord?

3. **2 Corinthians 12:12** — Truly the signs of an apostle were wrought among you in all patience, in signs, and wonders, and mighty deeds"

GREEK WORDS

1. "apostle" — **ἀπόστολος** (*apostolos*): a compound of **ἀπό** (*apo*) and **στέλλω** (*stello*); the word **ἀπό** (*apo*) means away, and the word **στέλλω** (*stello*) means "I send"; compounded, they form the word *apostolos*, which means one who is sent away; pictures a messenger, an envoy, or a delegate; one commissioned by another to represent him in some way; in the New Testament, it depicts a minister sent by Jesus Christ or by the Church; an apostle. The word **στέλλω** (*stello*) — the second part of the word "apostle" — is derived from **στολος** (*stolos*), which depicts a military expedition, a campaign, a tour, armed forces, army, navy, or a military entourage

2. "patience" — **ὑπομονή** (*hupomone*): to stay or abide; to remain in one's spot; to keep a position; to resolve to maintain territory gained; in a military sense, it pictures soldiers who maintain their positions even in the face of opposition; to defiantly stick it out regardless of pressures mounted against it; staying power; hang-in-there power; the attitude that holds out, holds on, outlasts, perseveres, and hangs in there, never giving up, refusing to surrender to obstacles, and turning down every opportunity to quit; one who is under a heavy load but refuses to bend, break, or surrender because he is convinced that the territory, promise, or principle under assault rightfully belongs to him

3. "signs" — **σημεῖον** (*semeion*): a proof; miracles

4. "wonders" — **τέρας** (*teras*): an event that leaves one baffled, bewildered, astonished; to be at a loss of words; depicts the shock, surprise, or astonishment felt by bystanders who observed events that were contrary to the normal course of nature; such occurrences were viewed as miracles, and people believed they could only take place through the intervention of divine power; these miraculous events left spectators speechless, shocked, astonished, bewildered, baffled, taken aback, stunned, awestruck, and in a state of wonder

5. "mighty deeds" — **δύναμις** (*dunamis*): explosive, superhuman power that comes with enormous energy and produces phenomenal, extraordinary, and unparalleled results; deeds that are impressive, incomparable, and beyond human ability to perform

SYNOPSIS

The Upper Room in the city of Jerusalem was not only the place where 120 of Jesus' disciples were baptized in the Holy Spirit on the Day of Pentecost (*see* Acts 2:1-4). It was also a rendezvous point that Jesus used for meeting with His apostles throughout His ministry. After hours of intense prayer, Jesus selected these 12 men to do ministry with and to be an extension of His ministry once He was gone. The role of the apostle was and is powerfully important.

The emphasis of this lesson:

In addition to the 12 men Jesus selected and appointed as apostles at the launching of His ministry, there are many other apostles mentioned in Scripture that God appointed and anointed to advance His Kingdom. The role of the apostle continues even to this day.

A Brief Review of Lesson 1

We saw in Lesson 1 that the word "apostle" is the Greek word *apostolos*. It is a compound of the word *apo*, meaning *away*, and the word *stello*, meaning *I send*. When you compound these two words, it forms the word *apostolos*; meaning *one who is sent away, a messenger, an envoy*, or *a delegate*. It is *one commissioned by another to represent him in some way*. In the New Testament, *it depicts a minister sent by Jesus Christ or by the Church*, and it is translated as the word "apostle."

We also noted that the word *stello* — the second part of the word *apostolos* — is derived from the word *stolos*, which depicts *a military expedition, a campaign, or a tour*; it pictures *armed forces, such as an army, a navy, or a military entourage*. Thus, apostolic ministry is *frontline ministry*. Like a military expedition that ventures into new territory to crush the enemy, apostles are highly trained individuals sent with God's power to crush the enemy and to take new territory for the Kingdom of God.

The word *apostolos* appears 79 times in the New Testament, and the word *apostello* — the term *apostolos* is derived from — appears no less than 131 times in the New Testament and more than 700 times in the Greek Septuagint. The fact that this word is used so frequently means it is very well established in Scripture.

Although it may seem that the word *apostolos* describes one that is disgraced and therefore dismissed, that is not the case. The word *apostolos* is a term of great honor that referred to a person who was personally selected, commissioned, and sent on an assignment on behalf of a very powerful government or individual. This person wasn't merely sent off; he was empowered, invested with authority, and dispatched to accomplish a special task.

In New Testament times, the word *apostolos* was also used in a variety of different ways. It described *the admiral of a fleet of ships*, a *passport* that guaranteed the right of passage, and an *ambassador* who represented another country. It was also employed to depict a person who was gifted by the gods and sent to the people as the gods' special messenger. Thus, an apostle of Jesus Christ was supernaturally gifted by God Himself with insights and abilities to establish the Church in new territories and take believers to places spiritually that they could probably never go to on their own. When believers in the First Century heard the word "apostle" — the Greek word *apostolos* — they understood all these things.

Who Are the 'Foundational Apostles'?

The first apostle is Jesus Himself. In fact, Jesus operated in all five of the fivefold ministry gifts. He was an Apostle, a Prophet, an Evangelist, a Pastor, and a Teacher. He is the perfect example of all five offices. Regarding His role as Apostle, Hebrews 3:1 says, "Wherefore, holy brethren, partakers of the heavenly calling, consider the Apostle and High Priest of our profession, Christ Jesus."

Thus, Jesus was the first Apostle, and then He chose 12 others to become apostles at the launching of His earthly ministry. These men are the *foundational apostles.* Matthew 10:2-4 says, "Now the names of the twelve apostles are these; The first, Simon, who is called Peter, and Andrew his brother; James the son of Zebedee, and John his brother; Philip, and Bartholomew; Thomas and Matthew the publican; James the son of Alphaeus, and Lebbaeus, whose surname was Thaddaeus; Simon the Canaanite, and Judas Iscariot, who also betrayed him."

These are the Twelve that Jesus chose. The criterion to be a foundational apostle was that the person had to have seen Jesus' ministry with his own eyes and have personally witnessed Jesus' resurrection. We know this to be true because Peter outlined it in the book of Acts when he and the other apostles were selecting a replacement for Judas Iscariot. After Judas committed suicide, the Bible says He was later replaced by Matthias who fit these qualifications (*see* Acts 1:15-26). He became one of the 12 foundational apostles — a very special group to which no one else will ever be added. They were eyewitnesses of Jesus' ministry and His resurrection.

What Other Apostles Are Named in the New Testament?

In addition to the Twelve, we read about other apostles in the New Testament. Thus, the word "apostle" is used in a broader sense. Here are the other apostles that are specifically named in the New Testament:

- **Paul** (Romans 1:1; 1 Corinthians 1:1; 2 Corinthians 1:1; Galatians 1:1; Ephesians 1:1; Colossians 1:1)
- **Apollos** (1 Corinthians 4:6-13)
- **Epaphroditus,** *apostolos* is translated as "messenger" (Philippians 2:25)
- **James,** the brother of Jesus (Galatians 1:19)
- **Barnabas** (Acts 14:4,14; 1 Corinthians 9:5,6)
- **Andronicus** (Romans 16:7)
- **Junia,** the wife of Andronicus (Romans 16:7)
- **Titus,** *apostolos* is translated as "messenger" (2 Corinthians 8:23)
- **An unnamed brother** with Titus (2 Corinthians 8:18, 23)
- **Another unnamed brother** with Titus (2 Corinthians 8:22,23)
- **Timothy** (1 Thessalonians 1:1; 2:6)
- **Silas** (1 Thessalonians 1:1; 2:6)

Although none of these people were foundational apostles, they did, nevertheless, function in the office of an apostle according to Scripture. With the exception of the apostle Paul and James, the foundational apostles were uniquely called to establish the Church universally and were the only ones anointed by God to write Scripture, which included the non-negotiable tenants of the Christian faith. They had a role that no one else had or will ever have.

By the end of the First Century, there were so many people claiming to be apostles it was creating a problem. Revelation 2:2 records that the Church of Ephesus began to "try" people who claimed to be apostles. The word "try" in Greek indicates the establishment of a tribunal to test and investigate people to confirm whether they were fake or authentic apostles. More than likely, there were many people that were calling themselves "apostles" who really didn't know the meaning of the word. They may have been highly gifted pioneers operating on the cutting edge of their field, but they were not genuine apostles.

According to the Bible, the function of a New Testament apostle includes:

- Those in the original group of 12 that were selected by Jesus and sent to lay the foundation of "the Universal Church" and to establish the non-negotiable apostolic doctrine. Paul would definitely be an exception to this, as he both wrote Scripture and started churches.

- Apostles in the broader sense — *including apostles today* — are called to establish churches in conjunction with the other fivefold gifts (prophets, evangelists, pastors, and teachers). They are also to undergird apostolic doctrines that were established by the original 12 apostles. No one is writing new doctrine. We are supporting and dispersing what has already been written.

The Criteria for Apostleship

Although Paul was not a member of the original Twelve, he was clearly an apostle. Having written nearly half of the New Testament and founding countless churches across the known world in the First Century, it seems he was in a category all by himself. Through him, the Holy Spirit established the criteria for true apostleship.

Number 1: *An apostle is one that has seen the Lord.* In First Corinthians 9:1 Paul stated, "Am I not an apostle? am I not free? have I not seen Jesus Christ our Lord? are not ye my work in the Lord?" The foundational apostles had certainly seen the Lord with their own eyes. Similarly, the apostle Paul saw the Lord, but it was in a vision while on the road to Damascus (*see* Acts 9:1-6). Like Paul, the other apostles also had visions of Christ and His Church. The only way Paul was able to construct the Church was to have his eyes supernaturally opened to see it.

Number 2: *An apostle is one that has patience.* In Second Corinthians 12:12 Paul said, "Truly the signs of an apostle were wrought among you in all patience, in signs, and wonders, and mighty deeds." Notice the very first thing Paul lists here as the sign of an apostle is *patience*. Although this may seem strange to list as a sign, it is not. Anyone that understands apostolic ministry knows that it does not take place in comfortable conditions. It is frontline ministry — a military expedition that pushes into new territory, fighting against the powers of darkness. If there was ever a virtue an apostle needed, it is patience.

The word "patience" is the Greek word *hupomone*, which means *to stay or abide; to remain in one's spot; to keep a position; to resolve to maintain territory gained*. In a military sense, it pictures *soldiers who maintain their positions even in the face of opposition*. It depicts one that defiantly sticks it out regardless of pressures mounted against it. It can also be described as *staying power* or *hang-in-there power; the attitude that holds out, holds on, outlasts, perseveres, and hangs in there, never giving up, refusing to surrender to obstacles, and turning down every opportunity to quit*. It is *a picture of one who is under a heavy load but refuses to bend, break, or surrender because he is convinced that the territory, promise, or principle under assault rightfully belongs to him*.

In other words, if you are called to be an apostle, you have to have supernatural endurance to stay put and not abandon ship when things get tough. By putting *patience* first, Paul insisted that it is one of the chief signs of apostleship. Only patience and endurance can give sufficient strength to keep a person pressing forward when it seems all of hell is raging against him.

Number 3: *An apostle is one that performs signs*. After patience, Paul added "signs" to the list of criteria for an apostle (*see* 2 Corinthians 12:12). The word "signs" is a translation of the Greek word *semeion*, which describes *a proof* or *miracles*. Paul's ministry and the ministry of the other apostles were marked by "signs." In Lystra, strength was restored to the limbs of a lame man (*see* Acts 14:8-10). In Philippi, demons were cast out of a woman (*see* Acts 16:16-18). Healing power was transferred through aprons or napkins taken from Paul's body to those who were bedridden and who couldn't attend his meetings because of their physical conditions (*see* Acts 19:11,12). In Troas, a young man was raised from the dead (*see* Acts 20:9-12), and in Melita, the sick were healed (*see* Acts 28:8-9).

Number 4: *An apostle is one that performs wonders*. Along with signs, Paul included "wonders" as proof for apostleship (*see* 2 Corinthians 12:12). The word "wonders" is the Greek word *teras*, which describes *an event that* *leaves one baffled, bewildered,* or *astonished.* It depicts *the shock, surprise, or astonishment felt by bystanders who observed events that were contrary to the normal course of nature.* Such occurrences were viewed as miracles, and people believed they could only take place through the intervention of divine power. These miraculous events left spectators speechless, shocked, astonished, bewildered, baffled, taken aback, stunned, awestruck, and in a state of wonder.

Number 5: *An apostle is one that performs mighty deeds.* In addition to signs and wonders, Paul stated that "mighty deeds" were the mark of apostleship (*see* 2 Corinthians 12:12). The phrase "mighty deeds" is a translation of the old Greek word *dunamis,* and it describes *explosive, superhuman power that comes with enormous energy and produces phenomenal, extraordinary, and unparalleled results.* It can also depict *the full force of an invading army.*

Although many people think that Paul and the other apostles experienced a non-stop flow of miraculous activity, that was not the case. A careful study of Paul's ministry, for instance, reveals that he had signs and wonders in his ministry at pivotal moments. Specifically, these supernatural demonstrations of the Holy Spirit's power manifested as he was bringing the Gospel into a new territory. These were spiritual military expeditions to drive out the powers of darkness. The signs, wonders, and mighty deeds were all evidence needed to verify that the message was authentic and true.

Keep in mind that the marks of an apostle Paul listed in Second Corinthians 12:12 are a good starting place in describing the signs that point to an apostolic call; they are not all-inclusive. Just as a highway sign lets you know you are coming close to a city, these particular signs in a person's ministry may be evidence that you're looking at a person who has a genuine apostolic call on his or her life.

In our next lesson, we will turn our attention to the role of a prophet and how to recognize the difference between those who are real and those who are counterfeit.

STUDY QUESTIONS

Study to shew thyself approved unto God, a workman that needeth
not to be ashamed, rightly dividing the word of truth.
— 2 Timothy 2:15

1. When you read through the description of the 12 foundational apostles that Jesus selected in Matthew 10:2-4, what unique connections do you notice about them? (Also consider Mark 3:13-19; Luke 5:27-29; 6:12-16; John 1:37-51.) What were the two must-have conditions for being a foundational apostle?
2. You probably know and have heard much about the apostle Paul, but did you know about all the other apostles mentioned in Scripture? Why do you think the Holy Spirit took the time to include these people?

PRACTICAL APPLICATION

> But be ye doers of the word, and not hearers only,
> deceiving your own selves.
> — James 1:22

1. One of the chief signs of apostleship is patience — *staying power* or *hang-in-there power, the attitude that holds out, holds on, outlasts, perseveres, and hangs in there, never giving up, refusing to surrender to obstacles, and turning down every opportunity to quit.* Have you ever experienced a time when this divine virtue was operating in your life?
2. If the answer is yes, what did it feel like when you received that supernatural strengthening? How did you know it occurred? What were the immediate, tangible results you experienced?
3. As you walk through your current challenges and difficulties, pray and ask the Holy Spirit to cultivate patience and strength into your character. Meditate on Isaiah 40:28-30 and make it a personalized prayer.

LESSON 3

TOPIC

The Ministry of the Prophet, Part 1

SCRIPTURES

1. **Ephesians 4:11** — And he gave some, apostles; and some, prophets; and some, evangelists; and some, pastors and teachers.

2. **Acts 11:27-28** — And in these days came prophets from Antioch. And there stood up one of them named Agabus, and signified by the Spirit that there should be a dearth throughout all the world: which came to pass during the days of Claudius Caesar.

3. **Acts 21:10,11** — And as we tarried there many days, there came down from Judaea a certain prophet, named Agabus. And when he was come unto us, he took Paul's girdle, and bound his own hands and feet, and said, Thus saith the Holy Ghost, So shall the Jews at Jerusalem bind the man that owneth this girdle, and shall deliver him into the hands of the Gentiles.

GREEK WORDS

1. "prophet" — προφήτης (*prophetes*): a compound of the words πρό (*pro*) and φημί (*phemi*); the word πρό (pro) is used in connection with phemi, which always means to say or to speak

2. "signified" — σημαίνω (*semaino*): to signify; to give a sign; to give an alert

3. "by" — διά (*dia*): through; through the instrumentality of

SYNOPSIS

Located in the Mount of Olives is an ancient tomb dating back over 2,500 years. In this amazing and mystical place, several of the Old Testament prophets were laid to rest, along with a number of their prophetic disciples. Although their bodies are no longer present in the tomb, their graves and the surrounding corridors have been well preserved.

Zechariah, who served as a prophet about 500 years before Christ, is one of the people that was buried here. Even though the engraving of his name has faded and is barely visible today, the majority of his prophecies have proven true. One prophecy — that the Messiah will return to the Mount of Olives at the end of the age — is still awaiting fulfillment. It is because of this prophecy that Zechariah and many other prophets were buried on the Mount of Olives.

As important as prophets were in the Old Testament, they are equally important in the New Testament. Understanding their role — then and now — is vital to understanding the fivefold ministry gifts Jesus gave to the Church. Paul tells us in Ephesians 4:11, "And he gave some, apostles; and some, prophets; and some, evangelists; and some, pastors and teachers." Just as there are present-day apostles, there are also present-day prophets, and we need to understand and welcome their ministry so we can receive this expression of Christ into our lives.

The emphasis of this lesson:

The ministry of the prophet is the second of the fivefold ministry gifts Christ gave to the Church. Prophets speak on behalf of God and bring a measure of Jesus to us that we would not have otherwise.

There Were Prophets in Both the Old and New Testaments

When you study the life of Jesus, you will clearly see that He stood in all five of the ministry gifts — He was an Apostle, an Evangelist, a Pastor, a Teacher, and a Prophet. All throughout the Old Testament, there were prophets of God — major and minor prophets and many prophets that are virtually unknown. Here are a few of the more well-known prophets from the Old Testament:

Noah, Abraham, Jacob, Joseph, Moses, Aaron, Miriam, Eldad and Medad, Elihu, Joshua, Deborah, Samuel, Saul, Gad, Nathan, David, Asaph, Heman, Jeduthun, Solomon, Agur, Ahijah, Iddo, Shemaiah, Azariah, Hanani, Jehu, Elijah, Micaiah, Jahaziel, Eliezer, Elisha, Jonah, Joel, Amos, Hosea, Isaiah, Micah, Obed, Zephaniah, Nahnum, Huldah, Jeremiah, Uriah, Habakkuk, Obadiah, Daniel, Ezekiel, Haggai, Zechariah, Malachi

There were many more prophets in the Old Testament through whom God spoke. There were also many prophets in New Testament times through whom God spoke. First and foremost, we know that Jesus was a prophet. Additionally, the Bible says that God prophesied through:

Simeon, Anna, John the Baptist, Paul, Barnabas, Lucius of Cyrene, Manaen, Simeon Niger, Judas, Silas, Paul, Timothy, Agabus, and Philip's four daughters

Although it may seem to be a small list, it is actually quite sizable, given the fact that the New Testament covers a much shorter span of time than the Old Testament.

What Does the Word 'Prophet' Mean?

Interestingly, the word prophet was a term generally used by all religions to describe any person that served as a voice for the spirit realm. For example, there were the pagan prophets of Baal, which Elijah encountered and defeated on Mount Carmel (*see* 1 Kings 18). Then there were the prophets of God that heard and spoke His messages to His people. Again, these were active in both Old and New Testament times, and there are still prophets today that are speaking God's voice.

The word "prophet" is a translation of the Greek word *prophetes*, which is a compound of the words *pro* and *phemi*. The word *pro* is used in connection with *phemi*, which always means *to say* or *to speak*. The word *phemi* lets us know this is a *speaking* or *saying gift*. The word *pro* — the first part of the word "prophet" — adds a wide range of meanings that are all critical to understanding a prophet's role.

Here are four specific ways the Greek word *pro* can be translated:

#1: The Greek word *pro* means *before*. It can describe a prophet's position *before* God.

Before the presence of God, a prophet listens with an open heart to whatever the Spirit of God would say to Him. But the word *phemi* — the second part of the word *prophetes* — shows that a prophet does more than listen; he listens and he *speaks*, conversing or communicating *before* the face of God. The prophet lingers in God's presence to receive clarification, making sure he understands the message God is speaking. This is the primary role of a prophet's responsibility.

So speaking and conversing *before* God is a requirement for him to fulfill his task. Many think that a prophet prophesies spontaneously, but in fact, if he speaks, he is able to speak because he has spent much time *before* the presence of God. He first speaks God's message *before* God to make sure he knows His heart and His message.

Although most think of a prophet's ability to prophesy, this is secondary to a prophet's primary function. The prophet's foremost task is to be in the presence of God to listen and hear His message clearly. He is humbling himself, lingering to clearly hear what God is saying.

Because the word "prophet" can be translated *to speak before*, it means foremost a prophet is to be *before* the Lord and to be *speaking before* Him. This pictures those moments when a prophet humbles Himself *before* the Lord and sensitizes his heart to the Lord's will and voice. As you will see, a prophet is like a sail on a sailboat — he cannot prophetically move unless he senses the wind of God's Spirit.

#2: The Greek word *pro* means *in front of*. It can describe a prophet's position *in front of* people.

A second translation of the word *pro* means *in front of*, and it depicts a prophet's public role to stand *in front of* people. The divine insights he receives from God are not for him; he is to impart them to those God asks him to stand *in front of*. He becomes the voice or mouthpiece of God. When the word *pro* is compounded with the word *phemi* — which means *to speak* — it means a prophet is called to public ministry *in front of* people.

Once he has heard and understands the message on God's heart, he moves from the solitary to the public to stand *in front of* (the Greek word, *pro*) people *to speak* (the Greek word, *phemi*). His job is to give the message God has authorized him to deliver and nothing more.

To be clear, a prophet cannot speak until the Holy Spirit moves across his spirit. Therefore, a prophet's first occupation is to be *before* the Lord in order to hear Him, to converse with Him, and to wait for the Spirit to move him to speak. As he waits for the moving of God's breath upon his own human spirit, he sets his spiritual sails to catch the wind of the Holy Spirit.

Once God has spoken to his heart and given him a message, and once he has been released by the Spirit of God to speak, then — finally — he is in a position to move into the next part of his ministry, which is to stand *in front of* people and speak God's message. This is public prophetic ministry.

#3: The Greek word *pro* means *on behalf of*. It can describe a prophet's responsibility to "speak on behalf of" the Lord.

The word *pro* can mean *on behalf of* and underscores that a prophet does not speak on his own behalf, or on the behalf of any other human being or organization. His job is *to speak* — the Greek word, *phemi* — but he does not have the right to speak his or anyone else's views or commentary or interpretation on a divine matter. He is to speak *on behalf of* the Lord and accurately represent His message. Thus, he is to be a clear channel with a clear message, and because he has humbled himself and caught the wind of God's Spirit, when he speaks, he will speak with a great anointing and with supernatural confirmation.

#4: The Greek word *pro* means *in advance*. It carries with it the sense of a predictive ability and can be translated as one who "speaks in advance."

The word *pro* can describe a prophet's ability *to speak* (the Greek word, *phemi*) with a certain predictive ability or to describe events *in advance* of their happenings. Although this is not what a prophet does all the time, it is a part of his ministry. This foretelling of events to come is clearly seen in both the Old and New Testament. Perhaps this is best illustrated in the New Testament by the example of the prophet Agabus.

Agabus: An Example of a New Testament Prophet

The prophet Agabus appears twice in the book of Acts. His first appearance is in Acts 11:27 and 28, which says, "And in these days came prophets from Antioch. And there stood up one of them named Agabus, and signified by the Spirit that there should be a dearth throughout all the world: which came to pass during the days of Claudius Caesar."

Notice the word "signified." It is the Greek word *semaino*, which means *to signify*, *to give a sign*, or *to give an alert*. It describes a foretelling of a coming event, and in this case, it was an advance notice that "a dearth [or famine] throughout all the world" was coming. This message Agabus gave was "by the Spirit." The word "by" is the Greek word *dia*, which means *through* or *through the instrumentality of*. Here, Agabus was enlightened and empowered to speak *through the instrumentality* of the Holy Spirit. Had he not been *before* the Lord in His presence, he would have had nothing *to speak* on the Lord's behalf.

In Acts 21:10 and 11, the prophet Agabus shows up a second time. The Bible says, "And as we tarried there many days, there came down from Judaea a certain prophet, named Agabus. And when he was come unto us, he took Paul's girdle, and bound his own hands and feet, and said, Thus saith the Holy Ghost, So shall the Jews at Jerusalem bind the man that owneth this girdle, and shall deliver him into the hands of the Gentiles."

Once again, we see the New Testament prophet Agabus moving in a predictive ability. Under the influence and moving of the Holy Spirit, he prophetically foretold what was about to happen to the apostle Paul when he arrived in Jerusalem. He would be bound and arrested and handed over to the Romans — all of which did come to pass as predicted. This is a clear example of a prophet's ability to *speak in advance* of things to come.

What About False Prophets?

If there is something real, you can rest assured the enemy will manufacture a counterfeit. Hence, just as there are real prophets, there are also *false* prophets. The same is true of apostles, evangelists, pastors, and teachers. There are those who are real and those who are fake. But don't get hung up on the phonies. Yes, they're out there, but if you become so afraid of being duped by a false prophet, you will become closed to the real ones and miss out on receiving what God has for you through them.

Think about it. Somewhere in society there is counterfeit money floating around. Fake twenties and hundreds are being produced and passed from place to place. But just because there are counterfeit bills out there doesn't mean you stay away from money. On the contrary, you need money and want more of it. Therefore, you do your best to make sure you have the real deal. The same principle applies to prophetic ministry.

With God's help you can learn to recognize who is a real prophet and who is a phony. In our next lesson, we will examine the biblical signs of a true prophet — what he does and what he will never do. Remember, Jesus gave prophets to the Church — which includes you — to be a portal of divine wisdom. If you are open, they can be a great gift of insight and direction for your life.

STUDY QUESTIONS

Study to shew thyself approved unto God, a workman that needeth not to be ashamed, rightly dividing the word of truth.
— 2 Timothy 2:15

1. Prior to this lesson, what was your understanding of a *prophet*? Did you have any misconceptions of what a prophet is? Have they been cleared up?

2. More than likely, you knew there were prophets in the Old Testament, but did you know there were prophets in the New Testament? What new insights have you acquired from this teaching about prophets?

3. As a believer, the Holy Spirit of Christ — the Prophet — lives in you! This means He can speak to you directly and show you things you could never know on your own. Jesus mentions this aspect of the Spirit's ministry in John 16:12-15. Take time to reflect on His words and share what the Holy Spirit speaks to you about His prophetic ability in your life. (Also consider 1 Corinthians 2:9,10; John 15:15; Psalm 25:12,14; Amos 3:7.)

PRACTICAL APPLICATION

But be ye doers of the word, and not hearers only, deceiving your own selves.
— James 1:22

1. Be honest. What has been your posture toward prophetic ministry? Have you been open or closed? Explain your answer.

2. By definition, a prophet is one who spends time *before* the Lord and then stands *in front of* people and *speaks* a message *on the Lord's behalf.* Who do you know that is functioning in the ministry of a prophet? In what specific ways has their gift impacted your life?

LESSON 4

TOPIC

The Ministry of the Prophet, Part 2

SCRIPTURES

1. **Ephesians 4:11** — And he gave some, apostles; and some, prophets; and some, evangelists; and some, pastors and teachers.

2. **2 Peter 1:20** — Knowing this first, that no prophecy of the scripture is of any private interpretation. For the prophecy came not in old time by the will of man: but holy men of God spake as they were moved by the Holy Ghost.

GREEK WORDS

1. "prophet" — προφήτης (*prophetes*): a compound of the words πρό (*pro*) and φημί (*phemi*); the word πρό (*pro*) is used in connection with phemi, which always means to say or to speak

2. "is of any private interpretation" — ἰδίας ἐπιλύσεως οὐ γίνεται (*idias epiluseos ou ginetai*): First, Peter uses ἰδίας (*idias*), which means of one's self. Second, Peter uses ἐπιλύσεως (*epiluseos*), a form of ἐπίλυσις (*epilusis*), which means to release or to loose. Third, Peter uses οὐ (*ou*), which means no. Fourth, Peter uses γίνεται (*ginetai*), which means to come to pass.

3. "moved" — φέρω (*phero*): to carry or to be borne along and it was used to depict ships that were carried along by the wind; in Acts 27:15 and 17, it denotes a ship whose sails were set to catch the wind

SYNOPSIS

As we saw in Lesson 3, there is a 2,500–year-old tomb located on the Mount of Olives. It was specifically constructed to be the burial site for the prophets Zechariah, Malachi, and Haggai. In the corridors surrounding these graves, many of their prophetic disciples were buried. Over the years, this place has become a sacred space where people gather regularly to meditate and pray. Indeed, the prophetic ministry in both the Old and New Testament has been and continues to be an important and a precious gift to the God's people.

The Bible tells us that after Jesus returned to Heaven, He gave the Church the fivefold ministry gifts, which are outlined in Ephesians 4:11. The apostle Paul wrote, "He gave some, apostles; and some, prophets; and some, evangelists; and some, pastors and teachers." In the original Greek, the text reads more emphatically. It says, "He gave some *indeed* to be apostles, some *indeed* to be prophets, some *indeed* to be evangelists, some *indeed* to be pastors, and some *indeed* to be teachers — no question about it."

The office of the prophet is the second of the fivefold ministry gifts. So prophetic ministry was not just for Old Testament times — it was for New Testament times, and it is also for us today. The question is, what role do prophets play in the Church? Is it the same as it was in times past, or is it different?

The emphasis of this lesson:

The primary task of a true prophet is to position himself before the presence of God. There in solitude, he learns how to hoist his spiritual sails and catch the wind of the Holy Spirit, speaking prophetically when God has something to say to His people.

A Brief Review of the Ministry of the Prophet

As we learned, the word "prophet" is a translation of the Greek word *prophetes*, which is a compound of the words *pro* and *phemi*. The word *pro* is used in connection with *phemi*, which always means *to say* or *to speak*. The word *phemi* lets us know the ministry of the prophet is a *speaking* or *saying gift*. The word *pro* — the first part of the word "prophet" — adds a wide range of meanings that are all critical to understanding a prophet's role.

There are four ways the Greek word *pro* can be translated. The first meaning we studied is *before*. It indicates that a prophet is *before* the Lord; he is both listening to the Lord and *speaking before* Him. This is his primary position and function. His eyes and ears are open to whatever God wishes to show him and say to him. He then *speaks before* God's presence for clarification, making sure he understands God's heart and the message He wants to convey.

Once the prophet has spent ample time *before* the Lord, he moves to the second phase of his ministry. This brings us to the second meaning of the word *pro*, which means *in front of*. This signifies that a prophet's role is a public one. The divine insights he has been given are for the sake of others. Once a prophet clearly understands God's message and he has been released by the Spirit to speak, he is dispatched to stand *in front of* people and deliver the word of the Lord.

The way in which the prophet delivers God's message is **on behalf of** the Lord. This is the third meaning of the word "pro." The word *pro* can mean *on behalf of* and it underscores that a prophet does not speak on his own behalf or on behalf of any other human being or organization. His job is *to speak* — the Greek word, *phemi* — but he does not have the right to speak his or anyone else's views, interpretations, or commentary on a divine matter. He is to speak *on behalf of* the Lord and accurately represent His message.

The fourth meaning of the word *pro* — the first part of the word *prophetes* — describes a prophet's ability **to speak in advance** with a certain predictive ability or to describe events *in advance* of their happenings. This foretelling of the prophet's ministry is clearly seen in both the Old and New Testament. Though a genuine prophet does not function in this "foretelling" all the time, he or she does move in this supernatural aspect of prophetic ministry from time to time.

How Prophets Do NOT Operate

During the First Century, discerning false prophets from true prophets was quite a challenge. For this reason, the apostle Peter took time in his second epistle to address this issue. He said, "Knowing this first, that no prophecy of the scripture is of any private interpretation" (2 Peter 1:20).

The phrase "knowing this first" is very emphatic in the Greek. It is as if Peter was saying, "Know this, know this, know this. Never forget what I'm about to say to you. It is of utmost importance." What did he want us to know first and foremost? "…That no prophecy of the scripture is of any private interpretation."

Now there are a number of people who misinterpret this verse. They believe it means we should never interpret one verse all by itself. Instead, we should always compare a verse with other verses to arrive at correct scriptural conclusions. Although this is a true and advisable principle when studying Scripture, it is not Peter's primary focus. In this verse, Peter was not talking about biblical interpretation. He was talking about how prophecy comes and telling his readers how prophetic ministry DOES and does NOT operate.

Again, when you look at this verse in the original Greek, it is quite different than how it reads in the *King James Version*. The phrase "is of any private interpretation" in Greek is *idias epiluseos ou genetai*. To understand what Peter is saying here, we must look at each word of this Greek phrase and discern its meaning.

First, Peter says, "of any." This is the Greek word *idias*, which means *of one's self*.

Second, he uses the phrase "private interpretation." This is a translation of the word *epiluseos*, which is a form of *epilusis*, and it means *to loose, to set free*, or *to release*. It depicts *a loosing or releasing of something at will.*

So the words "private interpretation" actually depict something that is *loosed* or *released by one's own self* — *at will.* And when the word *epilusis* is used with *idias*, it indicates something that is *self-willed* or *self-projected.* Thus, this part of the verse could be translated, *"no prophecy of the Scripture is self-willed or self-projected by one's own will."*

Next, Peter uses the word *ou*, which means *no, emphatically not.*

Lastly, he uses the word *genetai*, which describes *something that comes to pass.*

These two words together — *ou ginetai* — simply mean, *"it doesn't come to pass that way"* or *"it just doesn't happen like that."*

Putting the meanings of all these words together, here is the *Renner Interpretive Version (RIV)* for 2 Peter 1:20:

Knowing this first, that no prophecy of the scripture is self-willed or self-projected by one's own will – it simply doesn't happen that way!

This is a profoundly important scripture about how real prophetic ministry does *not* operate. Essentially, Peter said it is *not* self-produced, *not* self-willed, and *not* self-projected. True prophets don't have the power to freely loose something at their own will. They are directed by the Spirit of God and Him alone.

How Real Prophets DO Operate

Immediately after Peter told us how prophets do not operate, he tells us how they **do** operate. He said, "For the prophecy came not in old time by the will of man: but holy men of God spake as they were moved by the Holy Ghost" (2 Peter 2:21). The first part of this verse affirms everything we just gathered from verse 20 — that genuine prophecy is *not* self-produced nor does it come "by the will of man."

So then how does it come? Peter said it comes as, "…holy men of God spake as they were moved by the Holy Ghost" (2 Peter 2:21). The word "moved" is the Greek word *phero*, which means *to carry or to be borne along.* It was used to depict ships that were carried along by the wind. In Acts

27:15 and 17, it is specifically used to denote a ship whose sails were set to catch the wind.

The movement of ships was completely dependent upon the wind. But before a ship could catch the wind, the ship workers had to hoist the sails into position. By raising a ship's sails, the workers prepared the ship to move if the wind finally began to blow. The ship workers could not produce the wind… But they could prepare the sails to catch it when it began to blow.

This word "moved" — the Greek word *phero* — depicts a prophet that is raising his or her spiritual sails to catch the wind of the Spirit. And as a result, the Holy Spirit moves him along prophetically — like a ship that is propelled by the wind.

A real prophet, therefore, is one who spends a lot of time and energy in the presence of God sensitizing his spirit to God's Spirit. That is, he has learned to continually hoist his spiritual sails, making sure that he's in a position to catch the wind of the Spirit when the Spirit begins to move. Remember, a real prophet cannot self-project — he cannot speak anything on his own. He is totally dependent upon the wind of the Holy Spirit. When the wind of the Spirit blows, the prophet will be propelled and given prophetic movement. If God is not moving, there is no prophetic movement.

So while the prophet clearly has a speaking gift, this is not his primary task. His main duty is to spend a lot of time *before* the Lord in His presence. As he sits in solitude and prays in tongues, he prepares his spirit like the sails of a ship to catch the wind of the Spirit when God has something to say. When the Spirit begins to move, he senses it and opens his mouth to speak as the Spirit moves him along.

Just as there are times when a ship remains stationary, there will be seasons when there is no prophetic movement. When the wind of the Spirit ceases, the prophet cannot function. In the moments when the wind is not blowing, the prophet is waiting silently in the presence of God. In the stillness, there may be a temptation to fabricate something for the sake of excitement or to thrill a crowd, but this temptation must be resisted. Instead, he must listen for anything the Lord has to say and gathering clarification on anything he believes he has heard.

Again, a prophet's foremost task is to hoist his or her spiritual sails so that when God wants to speak, he or she will be in a position to catch the wind of the Holy Spirit and be "carried along" by the Holy Spirit and empowered to speak on God's behalf. If a prophet has not spent time preparing his heart and mind to catch the wind of God's Spirit, he will not see much divine activity. This means that a real prophet must be constantly in a time of preparation to catch the wind.

In our next two lessons, we will turn our attention to the ministry of the evangelist.

STUDY QUESTIONS

> Study to shew thyself approved unto God, a workman that needeth
> not to be ashamed, rightly dividing the word of truth.
> — 2 Timothy 2:15

1. Ephesians 4:11 clearly states that Jesus has *indeed* given us each expression of the fivefold ministry gifts. These include the ministry of the apostle, prophet, evangelist, pastor, and teacher. According to Ephesians 4:12 and 13, *why* have these gifts been given to the Church?

2. What can a real prophet *not* do on his own? What is he totally reliant upon in order to move in the prophetic? Why do you think this is so important?

3. Stop and think about the limitations of the prophet and what he needs to flow in his gifting. In what ways is your day-to-day life as a Christian similar? (As you answer consider Zechariah 4:6; John 15:4,5; and 2 Corinthians 3:5.)

PRACTICAL APPLICATION

> But be ye doers of the word, and not hearers only,
> deceiving your own selves.
> — James 1:22

1. Carefully read and reflect on Second Peter 1:20 and 21, along with Second Timothy 3:16 and 17. What connection(s) do you see between these passages, and how do they speak to you?

2. To help you identify and avoid listening to false prophets, check out these invaluable words from Peter and John in Second Peter 2:1-3 and First John 4:1-6. What is the Holy Spirit showing you in these verses?

TOPIC

The Ministry of the Evangelist, Part 1

SCRIPTURES

1. **Ephesians 4:11** — And he gave some, apostles; and some, prophets; and some, evangelists; and some, pastors and teachers.

2. **Luke 4:16-19** — And he came to Nazareth, where he had been brought up: and, as his custom was, he went into the synagogue on the sabbath day, and stood up for to read. And there was delivered unto him the book of the prophet Esaias. And when he had opened the book, he found the place where it was written. The Spirit of the Lord is upon me, because he hath anointed me to preach the gospel to the poor; he hath sent me to heal the brokenhearted, to preach deliverance to the captives, and recovering of sight to the blind, to set at liberty them that are bruised, to preach the acceptable year of the Lord.

GREEK WORDS

1. "evangelist" — εὐαγγελιστής (*euangelistes*): an evangelist; a bringer of good news; a crystal-clear channel for the spirit realm that allows spiritual communication to flow through

2. "upon" — ἐπί (*epi*): upon; on

3. "because" — ἕνεκεν (*heneka*): because; on account of; indicates purpose

4. "to preach the gospel" — εὐαγγελίσασθαι (*euangelisasthai*): to announce good news; to preach good news; to channel good news; to evangelize

5. "poor" — πτωχός (*ptochos*): pictures abject poverty; impoverished

6. "brokenhearted" — **συντρίβω** (*suntribo*): used to describe the crushing of grapes with the feet, or the smashing and grinding of bones into dust; depicts people who have been walked on by others, those who have been crushed by others, or those who feel they have been smashed to pieces by life or relationships

7. "heal" — **ἰάομαι** (*iaomai*): to cure; usually refers to a progressive cure; often depicts a healing power that progressively reverses a condition over a period of time, or a sickness that is progressively healed rather than instantaneously healed

8. "preach" — **κηρύσσω** (*kerusso*): to preach, proclaim, declare, announce, or herald a message

9. "deliverance" — **ἄφεσις** (*aphesis*): a release; a dismissal; to set free; to permanently loose

10. "captives" — **αἰχμάλωτος** (*aichmalotos*): captives; those taken captive at the point of a spear; those who are dragged into bondage; manipulated by bondage

11. "recovering of sight" — **ἀνάβλεψις** (*anablepsis*): the returning of one's sight; the restoration of sight; to see again

12. "blind" — **τυφλός** (*tuphlos*): blind; it doesn't just depict a person who is unable to see, but a person who has been intentionally blinded by someone else; can picture one whose eyes have been deliberately removed so that he is blinded; that individual hasn't just lost his sight, but he has no eyes with which to see

13. "set at liberty" — **ἄφεσις** (*aphesis*): a release; a dismissal; to permanently loose; to set free; in this case, from the detrimental effects of a shattered life; the Greek speaks of a permanent release from the destructive effects of brokenness

14. "bruised" — **τεθραυσμένους** (*tethrausmenous*): to crush; to break down; depicts a person who has been shattered or fractured by life; pictures those whose lives have been continually split up and fragmented

15. "acceptable" — **δεκτός** (*dektos*): favorable; accepted; a favorable time to receive

SYNOPSIS

The ancient city of Ephesus was a well-traveled place. People came from all across the Roman Empire — primarily by ship — to visit this coastal city in the province of Asia. As newcomers arrived, they took the harbor road and made their way into the heart of the city. This is how the apostle Paul and his ministry companions Aquila and Priscilla arrived in Ephesus in 52 A.D. They were carriers of the Gospel — the first evangelists — proclaiming the Good News of Jesus Christ into the midst of that pagan society.

The Bible says that when Jesus ascended into Heaven, "He gave some, apostles; and some, prophets; and some, evangelists; and some, pastors and teachers" (Ephesians 4:11). These are the fivefold ministry gifts that the Holy Spirit works through to bring spiritual maturity and growth to the Church, and the role of the *evangelist* is central to this work.

Many people today are confused about what an evangelist is and what he does. Contrary to what some believe, he is not someone who yells and screams and always preaches messages on the fires of hell and the wrath of God. Although messages like these are necessary, they are primarily communicated by a prophet. The main purpose of an evangelist is to present the Gospel in its purest form and allow the power of the Holy Spirit to confirm it as truth in ways that only He can.

The emphasis of this lesson:

The Bible gives us a clear picture of who an evangelist is and what he does. He is supernaturally equipped by God to be a carrier of the Good News and a clear channel of God's divine power.

What Is an Evangelist?

The word "evangelist" is a translation of the Greek word *euangelistes*. It is a compound of the word *eu*, which describes *something that is really good or swell*, and the word *angelos*, which is the New Testament word for *a messenger*. When these words are combined to form the word *euangelistes*, it describes *an evangelist, a bringer of good news*. This person is *a crystal-clear channel for the spirit-realm that allows spiritual communication to flow through him*.

Interestingly, the very earliest usage of the word "evangelist" is not in the Bible — it predates the New Testament. History reveals that the word "evangelist" was first used on a grave marker in a cemetery, and that grave marker commemorated the burial place of a famous medium. A medium is a person who channels [directs or guides] spirits and is a voice for the spirit realm. Originally, the word "evangelist" carried very negative connotations. However, when you take the idea of being a clear channel through whom spirits speak and you apply it in the context of the Kingdom of God, it provides a vivid picture of what an evangelist is and does.

Thus, an evangelist is supernaturally designed and equipped to be a channel of the Good News and God's divine power. When a person describes himself as an evangelist, he's actually saying, "I'm a channel through whom God speaks and through whom His supernatural power flows." When he brings his message and channels the power of God into a new environment, signs and wonders show up!

Jesus — the Ultimate Evangelist

Just as Jesus stood in the office of the apostle and the prophet, He also stood in the office of the evangelist. In fact, He was the first Evangelist. When we look at His life, we get a very vivid picture of who an evangelist is and what he does. Luke 4:16-19 provides us with this clear picture:

> **"And he came to Nazareth, where he had been brought up: and, as his custom was, he went into the synagogue on the sabbath day, and stood up for to read.**

> **And there was delivered unto him the book of the prophet Esaias [Isaiah]. And when he had opened the book, he found the place where it was written.**

> **The Spirit of the Lord is upon me, because he hath anointed me to preach the gospel to the poor; he hath sent me to heal the brokenhearted, to preach deliverance to the captives, and recovering of sight to the blind, to set at liberty them that are bruised, to preach the acceptable year of the Lord."**

The first thing Jesus said was, "The Spirit of the Lord is upon me...." The word "upon" is the Greek word *epi*, which literally means the Holy Spirit had come *upon* Him. The next word Jesus said was "because," and it is significant as it clarifies the *purpose* for which the Holy Spirit came upon Him. He didn't receive the fullness of the Holy Spirit just so He could experience a supernatural euphoria or feel good about Himself. There was a much higher purpose, and Luke 4:18 and 19 gives us six specific reasons.

#1: To Preach the Gospel to the Poor.

Interestingly, the phrase "to preach the gospel" is the Greek word *euange-lisasthai*, and it means *to announce good news; to preach good news; to channel good news; to evangelize.* In essence Jesus said, "I've been anointed with the Holy Spirit to *evangelize.*" Specifically, He said He was anointed to evangelize the "poor." The word "poor" is the Greek word *ptochos*, and it pictures *abject poverty or those who are impoverished.* This tells us the Gospel is good news for the poor. When an evangelist carries the Gospel to people in abject poverty, their economic status begins to change.

#2: To Heal the Brokenhearted.

The word "brokenhearted" is from the Greek word *suntribo* — a word that is used throughout the New Testament and the writings of the First Century. It was used to describe *the crushing of grapes with the feet,* or *the smashing and grinding of bones into dust.* It depicts *people who have been walked on by others, those who have been crushed by others, or those who feel they have been smashed to pieces by life or relationships.* Thus, the "broken-hearted" describes those who are emotionally shattered, tattered, and smashed.

Another important word in this verse is the word "heal." It is the Greek word *iaomai,* which literally means *to cure.* It usually refers to *a progressive cure* and *often depicts a healing power that progressively reverses a condition over a period of time* — *a sickness that is progressively healed rather than healed instantaneously.* This means that when an evangelist preaches the truth, he or she becomes a clear channel through which the power of God is released. If a person's heart has been smashed or crushed by others, God's power is discharged through the Good News, touching them on the spot and then progressively continuing to work in them until they are brought into a place of healing and wholeness.

#3: To Preach Deliverance to the Captives.

Notice the word "deliverance." It is the Greek word *aphesis,* which describes *a release* or *a dismissal.* It means *to set free* or *to permanently loose,* and this *release* or *permanent freedom* is to the "captives." The word "cap-tives" is the Greek word *aichmalotos,* and it describes *those taken captive at the point of a spear, those who are dragged into bondage* or *those manipulated by bondage.*

Think about how you would respond if your hands were bound and a person pressed a sharp spear between your shoulder blades. You would go wherever that spear directed you to go. This word "captives" pictures an outside force directing, manipulating, and forcing a person into bondage. Specifically, it represents any kind of addiction that enslaves and controls a person's life. When an evangelist shows up and proclaims the Good News, the Gospel message is released and with it the liberating power of God begins to flow. As a result, people who have been bound by addictions are instantaneously and permanently set free. This is a miraculous work of God through the evangelist.

#4: To Give Recovering of Sight to the Blind.

The phrase "recovering of sight" is a translation of the Greek word *anablepsis*, which means *the returning of one's sight; the restoration of sight;* or *to see again.* The word "blind" here is also very important. It is the Greek word *tuphlos,* which means *blind,* but it doesn't just depict a person who is unable to see. It depicts *a person who has been intentionally blinded by someone else. It can picture one whose eyes have been deliberately removed so that he is blinded; that individual hasn't just lost his sight, but he has no eyes with which to see.*

Second Corinthians 4:4 says that Satan, "...the god of this world hath blinded the minds of them which believe not...." This means those who don't believe don't even have eyes to see. When someone tries to share the Gospel with them, they just can't seem to grasp what is being said. The reason is they don't have eyes to see. But when an evangelist comes to preach, the power of God is released in such a way that spiritual eyes are created in those who are spiritually blind, and for the first time, they begin to see and hear and understand the truth. Clearly, an evangelist is a carrier of good news and power that brings wonderful results!

#5: To Set at Liberty Them That Are Bruised.

The fifth purpose Jesus — and all other evangelists — are anointed with the Spirit of God is to "set at liberty them that are bruised." The phrase "set at liberty" is once again the Greek word *aphesis,* and while it describes *a release* or *a dismissal,* in this case, *it indicates a permanent release from the detrimental effects of a shattered life.* Specifically, the Greek here speaks of a permanent release from the destructive effects of brokenness.

The word "bruised" in Greek means *to crush* or *to break down*. It depicts *a person who has been shattered or fractured by life; those whose lives have been continually split up and fragmented.* It is the exact same Greek word from where we get the word *trauma*. Thus, Jesus came to set at liberty — *to give a permanent release* — to people who have been traumatized by life. When a genuine evangelist shows up and begins to minister, this same type of restoration and freedom are discharged into the hearers who are hurting.

#6: To Preach the Acceptable Year of the Lord.

The final reason Jesus — and all other evangelists — are anointed with the Spirit of God is to "preach the acceptable year of the Lord." What's interesting about this portion of Scripture is that the word "year" doesn't appear in the Greek text. The word "acceptable" is the Greek word *dektos*, and it means *favorable* or *accepted*; it describes *a favorable time to receive.*

Hence, when an evangelist comes on the scene, it is a favorable time to receive from the Lord. He comes with a supernatural message, the supernatural equipment, and the supernatural power of God to bring real freedom and healing and restoration to the poor, the broken, the blind, and anyone that has been traumatized by life. These are the attributes that are clearly seen through the life of Jesus — the example of the ultimate evangelist.

STUDY QUESTIONS

Study to shew thyself approved unto God, a workman that needeth not to be ashamed, rightly dividing the word of truth.
— 2 Timothy 2:15

1. Before you began today's lesson, how did you envision an *evangelist?* What kind of responsibilities did you think he had? What type of messages did you think he preached? How do you see him differently now?

2. When you first heard the Good News of Jesus Christ, which category best describes your condition: the *poor*, the *brokenhearted*, the *captives*, the *blind*, or the *bruised?* Give reasons for your answer.

PRACTICAL APPLICATION

**But be ye doers of the word, and not hearers only,
deceiving your own selves.
—James 1:22**

1. Take a few moments to reflect on and briefly describe your salvation experience. What person (or people) was instrumental in sharing the Gospel with you?

2. What aspect of the Good News impacted your heart most — what did Jesus do that touched you most deeply and moved you to surrender your life to Him?

3. Jesus came to "set at liberty them that are bruised." This describes *a permanent release from the detrimental effects of a shattered life*. From what aspects of your shattered life did God grant you and immediate release? How did His divine power manifest in your life?

LESSON 6

TOPIC

The Ministry of the Evangelist, Part 2

SCRIPTURES

1. **Ephesians 4:11** — And he gave some, apostles; and some, prophets; and some, evangelists; and some, pastors and teachers.

2. **Luke 4:18,19** — The Spirit of the Lord is upon me, because he hath anointed me to preach the gospel to the poor; he hath sent me to heal the brokenhearted, to preach deliverance to the captives, and recovering of sight to the blind, to set at liberty them that are bruised, to preach the acceptable year of the Lord.

3. **Acts 6:8** — And Stephen, full of faith and power, did great wonders and miracles among the people

4. **Acts 8:4-6** — Therefore they that were scattered abroad went every where preaching the word. Then Philip went down to the city of Samaria, and preached Christ unto them. And the people with one

accord gave heed unto those things which Philip spake, hearing and seeing the miracles which he did.

5. **Acts 8:8** — And there was great joy in that city.

GREEK WORDS

1. "evangelist" — εὐαγγελιστής (*euangelistes*): an evangelist; a bringer of good news; a crystal-clear channel for the spirit realm that allows spiritual communication to flow through

2. "full" — πλήρης (*pleres*): full; full to capacity

3. "faith" — χάριτος (*charitos*): a form of χάρις (*charis*), the word for grace; in this verse, it pictures Stephen being full of χάρις (*charis*), which empowered him with δυνάμεως (*dunameos*) or with supernatural power

4. "power" — δυνάμεως (*dunameos*): a form of δύναμις (*dunamis*), the word for power or ability; depicts the assembled forces of an army whose combined strength enabled them to achieve unrivaled victories; these troops were so strong that they could not be resisted; generally, it depicts a power so mighty that it is impossible to resist or impossible to defeat

5. "great" — μεγάλα (*megala*): great; speaks of something enormous in quantity or quality

6. "wonders" — τέρας (*teras*): an event that leaves one baffled, bewildered, astonished; to be at a loss of words; depicts the shock, surprise, or astonishment felt by bystanders who observed events that were contrary to the normal course of nature; such occurrences were viewed as miracles, and people believed they could only take place through the intervention of divine power; these miraculous events left spectators speechless, shocked, astonished, bewildered, baffled, taken aback, stunned, awestruck, and in a state of wonder

7. "miracles" — σημεῖον (*semeion*): a sign; a mark or a token meant to verify or authenticate something; in the Greek world of the First Century AD, this word signified the official written notice that announced the final verdict of a court; also the signature or seal applied to documents to guarantee their authenticity; signs that marked key locations in a city; in the gospels, primarily depicts miracles and supernatural events that were intended to verify and authenticate the message of the Gospel

SYNOPSIS

The legendary city of Ephesus was a dark place filled with perversity and pagan practices. It was into this evil environment that the apostle Paul — along with his ministry associates Aquila and Priscilla — brought the Gospel in 52 AD and became the region's first *evangelists*.

The role of the evangelist is a vital part of the five-fold ministry gifts Christ gave the Church. Ephesians 4:11 says, "And he [Jesus] gave some, apostles; and some, prophets; and some, evangelists; and some, pastors and teachers." Although there are some similarities between these ministry gifts, each has its own uniqueness.

Like Paul, the apostle Philip also took on the role of an evangelist in the town of Samaria. Acts 8:5 and 6 says, "Then Philip went down to the city of Samaria, and preached Christ unto them. And the people with one accord gave heed unto those things which Philip spake, hearing and seeing the miracles which he did."

This passage illustrates what happens when an evangelist comes on the scene. In addition to bringing the Gospel message, he comes with the demonstration of the power of God. Signs, wonders, and miracles are his trademark. People not only hear the Good News with their ears, they also see the Good News in action with their eyes. The book of Acts is filled with these kinds of examples.

The emphasis of this lesson:

The Bible gives us clear examples of the role of an evangelist in the lives of Paul, Philip, Stephen, and Jesus — the Ultimate Evangelist. An evangelist is designed by God to be a clear channel through which the Good News and supernatural signs and wonders can flow.

A Brief Review of What We Know About an Evangelist

In our last lesson, we saw that the word "evangelist" is a compound of two Greek words: the word *eu*, which describes *something that is really good* or *swell*, and the word *angelos*, which is the New Testament word for *a messenger*. When these words are combined, they form the word *euangelistes*, which describes *an evangelist, a bringer of wonderfully good news — news that thrills and elate one's heart.*

The earliest use of the word "evangelist" predates the New Testament. It was found on a grave marker in a cemetery, and that grave marker commemorated the burial place of a famous medium in the occult. A medium is a person who channels spirits and is a voice for the spirit realm. When you take this understanding of a medium being a channel through whom spirits speak and apply it in the context of the Kingdom of God, it provides a vivid picture of what an evangelist is and does. He is *a crystal-clear channel for the Spirit of God to speak and flow through powerfully.*

A New Testament evangelist is supernaturally designed and equipped by God to be a channel through which the Good News and God's divine signs and wonders can flow. When a person describes himself as an evangelist, he's actually saying, "I'm a channel through whom God speaks and through whom His supernatural power flows." When he comes with his message and channels the power of God into a new environment, supernatural manifestations and miracles take place.

Jesus Provides Us a Perfect Picture of an Evangelist

In Luke 4:18 and 19, Jesus was standing in the synagogue in Nazareth, His boyhood town. As a visiting rabbi, He was given the opportunity to read from the Torah on that particular Sabbath. After being handed the book of the prophet Isaiah, He found the place where Isaiah prophesied about Him saying:

> "The Spirit of the Lord is upon me, because he hath anointed me to preach the gospel to the poor; he hath sent me to heal the brokenhearted, to preach deliverance to the captives, and recovering of sight to the blind, to set at liberty them that are bruised, to preach the acceptable year of the Lord."

Jesus was the perfect Evangelist, and in this passage, He described in detail the role of the New Testament evangelist. We saw in our last lesson that an evangelist does not preach about the fire and brimstone judgment of God. Instead, he preaches the Good News of Jesus Christ and all the Gospel entails.

The first responsibility of an evangelist that Jesus noted was to **preach the Gospel to the poor**. This means his message is so powerful and so filled with good news that if impoverished, poverty-stricken people hear and believe it, it will begin to change their economic status. That is good news!

Second, Jesus said that as an evangelist, He was sent to *heal the brokenhearted*. The first part of the word "brokenhearted" in this phrase is the word *suntribo*, and it describes those *people who have been walked on by others, those who have been crushed by others, or those who feel they have been smashed to pieces by life or relationships*. When an evangelist shows up and preaches the Good News, divine power is released that begins to progressively "heal" — from the Greek word *iaomai* — those who are brokenhearted, putting their lives back together again.

The third function of an evangelist is *to preach deliverance to the captives*. The word "deliverance" is the Greek word *aphesis,* and it describes *a permanent release* or *a permanent dismissal* for those who are captives. The word "captives" here describes *those taken captive at the point of a spear, those who are dragged into bondage* or *those manipulated by bondage*. Specifically, it represents any kind of addiction that enslaves and controls a person's life.

When an evangelist comes, he is such a clear channel for the power of God that virtue begins to flow through him and bring permanent release and deliverance to people that are held hostage by any kind of addiction — whether it be the chemical addiction of drugs or the sexual addiction of pornography, adultery, or homosexuality. The evangelist comes with liberating power to instantaneously set people free once and for all.

The fourth mark of an evangelist described by Jesus is that he brings *recovering of sight to the blind*. The word "blind" here is the Greek word *tuphlos*, and it doesn't just describe someone that can't see. It's depicts *someone who's eyes have been intentionally gouged out by someone else*. This individual hasn't just lost his sight; he has no spiritual eyes with which to see. But when an evangelist comes and begins to preach, he brings *"recovering of sight"* to those who have no eyes to see. The phrase "recovering of sight" is a translation of the Greek word *anablepsis*, which means *the returning of one's sight, the restoration of sight*, or *to see again*.

Second Corinthians 4:4 says that Satan, "...the god of this world hath blinded the minds of them which believe not...." This indicates that those who don't believe in Jesus don't even have eyes to see. If you try to share the Gospel with them, they just can't seem to understand what is being said. Satan has gouged out their spiritual eyes, so they can't see. But when an evangelist comes to preach, the power of God is released in such a way that spiritual eyes are created in those who are spiritually blind, and for the first time, they are able to see and understand the glorious Gospel of

Jesus Christ. Clearly, an evangelist is a carrier of good news and power that brings wonderful results!

The fifth characteristic of an evangelist according to Luke 4:18 is the divine ability **to set at liberty them that are bruised.** The phrase "set at liberty" is again the Greek word *aphesis*, which in this case describes *a permanent release* or *a permanent dismissal from the detrimental effects of a bruised life*. The Greek word for "bruised" is from where we get the word *trauma*. It depicts *a person who has been shattered or fractured by life; those whose lives have been continually split up and fragmented.* When an evangelist preaches the Good News, he becomes a clear stream of God's Power, and those that have been traumatized by troubling relationships and disastrous events have their lives supernaturally put back together again.

The sixth quality of an evangelist Jesus included in Luke 4:19 is the divine ability **to preach the acceptable year of the Lord.** What's interesting about this verse is that the word "year" doesn't appear in the original Greek text. The word "acceptable" is the Greek word *dektos*, and it means *favorable* or *accepted*; it describes *a favorable time to receive*. The use of this word indicates that when an evangelist shows up, it is a favorable season for everyone in attendance. The power of God is going to be in operation, bringing the Good News and supernatural results.

Stephen Was an Evangelist in Judea

In addition to Jesus, the Bible provides us with many examples of an evangelist, including a man named Stephen. Although he began as a deacon, distributing food provisions to widows and those in need, the Holy Spirit quickly promoted him to the position of an evangelist in the city of Jerusalem.

Acts 6:8 says, "And Stephen, full of faith and power, did great wonders and miracles among the people." The word "full" here is the Greek word *pleres*, which means *full* or *full to capacity*. But when we come to the word "faith," we run into a problem with the translation. The King James Version uses the word "faith," but the Greek text uses the word *charitos*, which is a form of the Greek word *charis*, the New Testament word for *grace*. Hence, this verse literally says Stephen was full of *grace* (*charis*).

It also says he was full of "power," which is the Greek word *dunameos*, a form of the word *dunamis*. This word describes supernatural power or ability. It depicts *the assembled forces of an army whose combined strength enabled them to achieve unrivaled victories. These troops were so strong that they could not be resisted.* In a general sense, it depicts *a power so mighty that it is impossible to resist or impossible to defeat.*

This means Stephen, the evangelist, was full of *grace (charitos)*, and that *grace* provided such empowerment that divine power *(dunamis)* was released through him. It was as if the armies of Heaven showed up on the scene and began driving out sickness and disease. The enemy could not resist the supernatural strength flowing out from Stephen when he began preaching the Good News.

Through the empowerment of God's grace, the Bible says he "...did great wonders and miracles among the people" (Acts 6:8). The word "great" is the Greek word *megala*, which speaks of something enormous in quantity or quality. The word "wonders" is the Greek word *teras*, and it describes *an event that leaves one baffled, bewildered, or astonished*; to be at a loss of words. It depicts *the shock, surprise, or astonishment felt by bystanders who observed events that are contrary to the normal course of nature.* Such occurrences were viewed as miracles, and people believed they could only take place through the intervention of divine power. These miraculous events left spectators speechless, shocked, astonished, bewildered, baffled, taken aback, stunned, awestruck, and in a state of wonder.

In addition to "wonders," Stephen's ministry of evangelism was marked by "miracles" — the Greek word *semeion*, which describes *a sign, a mark, or a token meant to verify or authenticate something.* In the Greek world of the First Century AD, this word signified the official written notice that announced the final verdict of a court; the signature or seal applied to documents to guarantee their authenticity; or even signs that marked key locations in a city. In the gospels, the word *semeion* — translated here as "miracles" — primarily depicts miracles and supernatural events that were intended to verify and authenticate the message of the Gospel.

These "miracles" were God's signature — His seal of approval — that the Gospel message being presented was the real deal.

Philip Was an Evangelist in Samaria

When we move to Acts chapter 8, we find another evangelist at work — the evangelist named Philip. As a result of great persecution that came upon the Church, the Bible says, "Therefore they that were scattered abroad went every where preaching the word. Then Philip went down to the city of Samaria, and preached Christ unto them" (Acts 8:4,5).

Notice that Philip, the evangelist, preached "Christ unto them." He didn't preach about Hell, fire, and God's wrath. He preached the Good News of Jesus Christ. God was using Philip to create spiritual eyes in the spiritually blind people of Samaria so they could see and understand the redeeming message of the Gospel.

What were the results? Verse 6 says, "And the people with one accord gave heed unto those things which Philip spake, hearing and seeing the miracles which he did." This is a classic example of what happens when an evangelist shows up. He provides divine proof that people can both hear and see. Specifically, the Bible says that Philip did "miracles," which is once again the Greek word *semeion*, describing *a sign, a mark, or a token meant to verify or authenticate something as being real.*

Just as God had designed Stephen to be a channel of divine power, He designed Philip in the same way. As he preached the Good News, the power (*dunamis*) of God began to flow through him to authenticate the message. Consequently, the powers of darkness were driven back and people were set free from debilitating diseases and addictions. As a result, the Bible says, "There was great joy in that city" (Acts 8:8). That is what an evangelist's anointed efforts produce — great joy and supernatural change in people's lives.

Although it's been nearly two thousand years since Philip and Stephen served as evangelists, God has continued to raise up men and women to carry out the work of this office. People like Oral Roberts, T.L. Osborn, and Kathryn Kuhlman were all New Testament evangelists. They came preaching the Good News of Jesus Christ, and when they did, the power of God showed up! These individuals were crystal-clear channels for the supernatural power of God to flow, producing miraculous healings, numerous salvations, and great joy among the people. Indeed, the gift of the evangelist is a true blessing we need in the Church today.

STUDY QUESTIONS

Study to shew thyself approved unto God, a workman that needeth not to be ashamed, rightly dividing the word of truth.
— 2 Timothy 2:15

1. According to Romans 1:16, what kind of impact does the Gospel have on people? What does God say we can and should expect when His Word is proclaimed? (*See* Hebrews 4:12; James 1:21.)

2. Second Corinthians 4:4 says that Satan, "...the god of this world hath blinded the minds of them which believe not...." Who do you know and care for deeply that has had their spiritual eyes intentionally gouged out by the enemy?

3. In Acts 26:18, Paul described his calling as an evangelist to the Gentiles and revealed God's will for those who are unsaved. Take a few moments to reflect on this verse and turn it into a prayer for your unsaved loved ones — that their eyes would be opened to the truth. (Also *consider* 2 Kings 6:16,17.)

PRACTICAL APPLICATION

**But be ye doers of the word, and not hearers only,
deceiving your own selves.
— James 1:22**

1. Do you know anyone who fits the description of a modern-day, New Testament evangelist? (Maybe it is someone you had mistakenly placed into another category of the five-fold ministry gifts.) Is this possibly a gift in which you yourself are anointed to flow?

2. Can you remember the moment God blessed you and gave you spiritual eyes to see the truth of the Gospel? What was your response to seeing and understanding the mercy and grace of God and the forgiveness of sin through faith in Jesus Christ, His Son?

LESSON 7

TOPIC

The Ministry of the Pastor, Part 1

SCRIPTURES

1. **Ephesians 4:11** — And he gave some, apostles; and some, prophets; and some, evangelists; and some, pastors and teachers.

2. **John 10:11** — I am the good shepherd: the good shepherd giveth his life for the sheep.

3. **Ezekiel 34:1-12, 14-16** — And the word of the Lord came unto me, saying, Son of man, prophesy against the shepherds of Israel, prophesy, and say unto them, Thus saith the Lord God unto the shepherds; Woe be to the shepherds of Israel that do feed themselves! should not the shepherds feed the flocks? Ye eat the fat, and ye clothe you with the wool, ye kill them that are fed: but ye feed not the flock. The diseased have ye not strengthened, neither have ye healed that which was sick, neither have ye bound up that which was broken, neither have ye brought again that which was driven away, neither have ye sought that which was lost; but with force and with cruelty have ye ruled them. And they were scattered, because there is no shepherd.... My sheep wandered through all the mountains, and upon every high hill: yea, my flock was scattered upon all the face of the earth, and none did search or seek after them. Therefore, ye shepherds, hear the word of the Lord, As I live, saith the Lord God, surely because my flock became a prey, and my flock became meat to every beast of the field, because there was no shepherd, neither did my shepherds search for my flock, but the shepherds fed themselves, and fed not my flock. Therefore, O ye shepherds, hear the word of the Lord, Thus saith the Lord God; Behold, I am against the shepherds; and I will require my flock at their hand, and cause them to cease from feeding the flock; neither shall the shepherds feed themselves any more; for I will deliver my flock from their mouth, that they may not be meat for them. For thus saith the Lord God; Behold, I, even I, will both search my sheep, and seek them out. As a shepherd seeketh out his flock in the day that he is among his sheep that are scattered; so will I seek out my sheep, and [I] will deliver them out of all places where they have been scattered in the cloudy and dark day. I will feed them in a good pasture, and upon the high mountains of Israel shall their fold be: there shall they lie in a good fold, and in a fat pasture shall they feed upon the mountains of Israel. I will feed my flock, and I will cause them to lie down, saith the Lord God. I will seek that which was lost, and bring again that which was driven away, and will bind up that which was broken, and will strengthen that which was sick: but I will destroy the fat and the strong; I will feed them with judgment."

GREEK WORDS

1. "the good shepherd" — ὁ ποιμὴν ὁ καλός (*ho poimen ho kalos*): ὁ ποιμὴν (ho poimen) refers to the shepherd — the feeder, protector, and the ruler of a flock of men; ὁ καλός (*ho kalos*) refers to the good one; the most excellent one; the one who is the supreme example

2. "giveth" — τίθημι (*tithemi*): to place; to lay down; to establish

3. "life" — ψυχή (*psuche*): soul; mind, will, and emotions; hence, one's human life

4. "for" — ὑπὲρ (*huper*): on behalf of

5. "sheep" — πρόβατον (*probaton*): especially a sheep in the New Testament

SYNOPSIS

Just outside of the city of Bethlehem are the ancient hillside ruins where shepherds used to tend their sheep. Although people in society didn't have a very high opinion of shepherds, there job was important. In fact, God viewed them as a valuable part of His redemptive plan. Remember, it was to the shepherds that the angels first appeared and announced the Savior's birth. They became the first evangelists to tell others the Good News of Jesus' arrival.

The truth is, pastors are a lot like shepherds. They are one of the fivefold ministry gifts Christ gave the Church. In Ephesians 4:11, our anchor verse, it says, "And he [Jesus] gave some, apostles; and some, prophets; and some, evangelists; and some, pastors and teachers." It's interesting to note that the word for "pastors" in the New Testament — including here in this verse — is the Greek word *poimen*, which is the word for "shepherds."

Just as Jesus stood in the office of apostle, prophet, and evangelist, He also stood in the role of the pastor, or shepherd. In John 10:11, He said, "I am the good shepherd...." The phrase "the good shepherd" in Greek is *ho poimen ho kalos*. The words *ho poimen* refers to *the shepherd, the feeder, the protector*, and *the ruler of a flock of men*. The Greek includes the definite article, which indicates that Jesus is the Shepherd above all shepherds. And the words *ho kalos* refers to *the good one, the most excellent one, the one that is the supreme example*. Thus, Jesus is the best example of what a shepherd — or *pastor* — should be.

The emphasis of this lesson:

The role of the pastor is one of the fivefold ministry gifts Christ gave to the Church, and it is vital to the Church's strength and maturity. The pastor's primary purpose is to regularly feed the congregation healthy spiritual food.

How Did Jesus Describe a Good Pastor?

In the second part of John 10:11, Jesus went on to say, "...The good shepherd giveth his life for the sheep." The word "giveth" here is a form of the Greek word *tithemi*, which in this case means *to place, to lay down*, or *to establish*. Thus, the first thing Jesus said that a good shepherd — or a good pastor — does is lay down his life for the sheep, which are the people he pastors. He does this in order *to establish* them in the principles of God's Word.

The word "for" is also significant in this verse. When Jesus said "...the good shepherd giveth his life *for* the sheep," the word "for" is the Greek word *huper*, which means *on behalf of*. Hence, a good pastor is one who gives, invests, or lays down his life *on behalf of* others. The word "sheep" is used to describe a flock of sheep, which of course refers to the Church. This word "sheep" in Greek is the word *probaton*, which means *especially a sheep in the New Testament*.

Jesus was the supreme example of what a pastor should be. He went so far as to give His life for us, His sheep. Interestingly, the word "life" is the Greek word *psuche*, which is from where we get the words *psyche* and *psychology*. It describes *the mind, the will, and the emotions*. The use of this word signifies all that is involved in pastoral ministry. A good pastor dedicates the fullness of his life — his mind, will, and emotions — to his God-given responsibilities.

Jesus ultimately gave His life for us. Of His own free will, He laid it down and surrendered to the will of the Father. But He didn't just suffer horrific beatings and endure the death of the Cross to pardon our sins. He sacrificed His life in order to establish us on a good foundation of faith, and that should be the goal of every pastor.

God Gives a Clear Picture of What Pastors Are To Do

In Ezekiel 34, God spoke some very strong words of correction to the shepherds of Israel. These spiritual leaders were failing miserably in their responsibilities. As we read His rebuke, we can learn very specifically what a shepherd — or pastor — is supposed to do by what God corrected them for *not* doing.

Ezekiel 34:1-3 says, "And the word of the Lord came unto me, saying, Son of man, prophesy against the shepherds of Israel, prophesy, and say unto them, Thus saith the Lord God unto the shepherds; Woe be to the shepherds of Israel that do feed themselves! should not the shepherds feed the flocks? Ye eat the fat, and ye clothe you with the wool, ye kill them that are fed: but ye feed not the flock."

In these three verses, we see God correcting the shepherds twice for not "feeding the flocks." He mentions this again and again throughout this chapter, which indicates that **the primary responsibility of a pastor (shepherd) is to provide spiritual nourishment for the sheep**. God is not against a pastor feeding and clothing himself or being blessed. But He is against pastors only being concerned for their own needs and not doing what He has called them to do.

God went on to say, "The diseased have ye not strengthened, neither have ye healed that which was sick, neither have ye bound up that which was broken, neither have ye brought again that which was driven away, neither have ye sought that which was lost; but with force and with cruelty have ye ruled them" (Ezekiel 34:4). Here we see five specific things the shepherds of Israel had *failed* to do:

1. **The diseased ye have not strengthened.**
2. **Neither have ye healed that which was sick.**
3. **Neither have ye bound up that which was broken.**
4. **Neither have ye brought again that which was driven away.**
5. **Neither have ye sought that which was lost.**

By hearing what these shepherds — or pastors — were *not* doing, we can determine what pastors should be doing.

1. **Pastors are to strengthen the diseased.** This means pastors are to nurture, encourage, and strengthen those who are struggling with issues of sin or any other area of their life.

2. **Pastors are to heal those that are sick.** The word "sick" here can refer to those who are physically or spiritually ill. This means pastors have a responsibility to help bring healing to people who are sick in their souls and bodies.

3. **Pastors are to bind up those that are broken.** Sheep have a propensity to get hurt and even break a leg. It was the responsibility of the shepherd to make a splint for the wounded sheep and help them heal. In the same way, pastors have a responsibility to bind up people who are broken by life — broken in their marriage, their finances, or their relationships — and help them mend.

4. **Pastors are to bring again those who were driven away.** There are many people who experience hurt in church. They don't understand why things happened the way they did or why certain decisions were made, and they become disappointed or offended and leave. Rather than say, "Good riddance," pastors have a level of responsibility to go after and find people who have wandered away and encourage them back into the congregation.

5. **Pastors are to seek those who are lost.** There are people in the church as well as outside the church who are lost. Pastors have a responsibility to reach out and make every effort to rescue those that are without Christ and are perishing.

After God pointed out all the areas where the pastors of Israel were falling short, He told them "…with force and with cruelty have ye ruled them [the people of Israel]" (Ezekiel 34:4). Although God is not against pastors leading and ruling the church for which they are responsible, He is against them neglecting or abusing His people.

What Happens to Pastors Who Refuse To Do Their Job?

God continued to reprimand the shepherds of Israel by saying, "And they were scattered, because there is no shepherd…. My sheep wandered through all the mountains, and upon every high hill: yea, my flock was scattered upon all the face of the earth, and none did search or seek after them" (Ezekiel 34:5,6).

The reason the "sheep" had wandered off was because the shepherds were not doing their job. To make matters worse, the shepherds didn't go after the ones who were scattered. This tells us that when pastoral leadership is lacking, people begin to wander off into wrong places. However, when there is strong pastoral leadership, it serves to help hold the "flock" together.

Speaking through the prophet Ezekiel, God went on to say, "Therefore, ye shepherds, hear the word of the Lord, As I live, saith the Lord God, surely because my flock became a prey, and my flock became meat to every beast of the field, because there was no shepherd, neither did my shepherds search for my flock, but the shepherds fed themselves, and fed not my flock. Therefore, O ye shepherds, hear the word of the Lord, Thus saith the Lord God; Behold, I am against the shepherds; and I will require my flock at their hand, and cause them to cease from feeding the flock; neither shall the shepherds feed themselves any more; for I will deliver my flock from their mouth, that they may not be meat for them" (Ezekiel 34:7-10).

Twice more in this passage, God chastised the shepherds of Israel for not feeding His sheep and only feeding themselves — punctuating the fact that **the primary responsibility of a pastor (shepherd) is to provide spiritual nourishment for the sheep.** For their continued irresponsibility, God said He was against them and would take the flock and give them to someone else that would care for them correctly.

God Himself Will Become a Shepherd to Those Being Neglected

After God pointed out to the shepherds of Israel their shortcomings, He shifted gears and made a promise to the sheep that had been ignored and abandoned: "For thus saith the Lord God; Behold, I, even I, will both search my sheep, and seek them out. As a shepherd seeketh out his flock in the day that he is among his sheep that are scattered; so will I seek out my sheep, and [I] will deliver them out of all places where they have been scattered in the cloudy and dark day. I will feed them in a good pasture, and upon the high mountains of Israel shall their fold be: there shall they lie in a good fold, and in a fat pasture shall they feed upon the mountains of Israel. I will feed my flock, and I will cause them to lie down, saith the Lord God. I will seek that which was lost, and bring again that which was driven away, and will bind up that which was broken, and will strengthen that which was sick: but I will destroy the fat and the strong; I will feed them with judgment" (Ezekiel 34:11,12, 14-16).

In these five verses, the Lord tells the irresponsible shepherds, "If you won't do the job of pastoring My people, I will do it Myself! I Myself will strengthen the diseased, heal those that are sick, bind up those that are broken, bring again those that have been driven away, and seek out those that are lost. I'm going to bring My sheep — my people — into a good, safe pasture where they can lie down in a good fold without fear."

Every good pastor should desire and aim at feeding and protecting the spiritual flock that has been entrusted to him. He should also seek to lead them into "high places," which signifies bringing them into new, higher spiritual levels. This is the heart of God for His people.

Christ gave the Church "pastors" — the Greek word *poiman* — to serve as shepherds of His sheep. Every pastor is to be a *provider*, a *protector*, and a *ruler in their local congregation*. They have been entrusted by God with a very high position and given the responsibility to care for God's people in these specific ways. As we wrap up this lesson, here are seven specific duties of a good pastor:

Seven Duties of a Good Shepherd for His Sheep

1. He knows the state of his sheep (or congregation).
2. He knows how to nourish, feed, and reprove the sheep to bring them into a state of spiritual soundness.
3. He knows how to rescue and restore the sheep who have fallen into sin.
4. He knows how to find the sheep who have been driven away.
5. He knows how to bring sheep back into the fold who have strayed into strange pastures.
6. He knows how to oppose and expel wolves who have gotten in among the sheep and are scattering them from each other and from God.
7. He knows how to preach, explain, and defend the truth for the sheep.

STUDY QUESTIONS

Study to shew thyself approved unto God, a workman that needeth not to be ashamed, rightly dividing the word of truth.
— 2 Timothy 2:15

1. Without question, pastors are very important to the spiritual growth and well-being of the Church. Prior to this lesson, what was your

perception of the role of a pastor? How has your understanding been expanded and/or redirected?

2. Hebrews 13:17 is a powerful verse giving clear instruction on how we are to treat our pastors. According to this passage, what is one of the most important things God wants you to do for your pastor? For what sobering reason(s) are you to act this way?

PRACTICAL APPLICATION

**But be ye doers of the word, and not hearers only,
deceiving your own selves.
—James 1:22**

Every trip to the doctor usually starts with a check of your vital signs to assess your level of health. Take a few moments to answer the following questions in order to evaluate the level of honor you are giving to your pastor.

1. How would you describe your attendance: *regular, random,* or *hardly ever?*

2. How about your punctuality? Are you usually *a little early, on time,* or *late?*

3. How often would you say that you pray for your pastor and his family: *often, sometimes,* or *never?*

4. How would you describe your words about your pastor to others? *Positive and supportive* or *negative and critical?*

5. When your pastor is teaching, are you *leaning in and taking in* what he's saying, or is your mind *preoccupied with other things?*

6. If your pastor asks the congregation — which includes you — for help in a certain area, do you look for ways you can help, or do you look for excuses to exempt you from having to help?

7. In light of your answers, would you say that you are *honoring* your pastor by your actions or *dishonoring* him? If you answered dishonoring, take time now to repent and ask God to forgive you and give you a heart of honor for the person He has provided to be your shepherd.

TOPIC

The Ministry of the Pastor, Part 2

SCRIPTURES

1. **Ephesians 4:11** — And he gave some, apostles; and some, prophets; and some, evangelists; and some, pastors and teachers.

2. **John 10:11** — I am the good shepherd: the good shepherd giveth his life for the sheep.

3. **Acts 20:28** — Take heed therefore unto yourselves, and to all the flock, over the which the Holy Ghost hath made you overseers, to feed the church of God, which he hath purchased with his own blood.

4. **1 Peter 5:1-4** — The elders which are among you I exhort, who am also an elder, and a witness of the sufferings of Christ, and also a partaker of the glory that shall be revealed. Feed the flock of God which is among you, taking the oversight thereof, not by constraint, but willingly [according to God]; not for filthy lucre, but of a ready mind. Neither as being lords over God's heritage, but being ensamples to the flock. And when the chief Shepherd shall appear, ye shall receive a crown of glory that fadeth not away

GREEK WORDS

1. "the good shepherd" — **ὁ ποιμὴν ὁ καλός** (*ho poimen ho kalos*): **ὁ ποιμὴν** (ho poimen) refers to the shepherd — the feeder, protector, and the ruler of a flock of men; **ὁ καλός** (*ho kalos*) refers to the good one; the most excellent one; the one who is the supreme example

2. "take heed" — **προσέχω** (*prosecho*): giving one's full attention to what is being spoken and heard and drawing as near to it as possible; to give one's full attention to a matter; to apply the mind to a thing; to give serious consideration and contemplation to what is being heard

3. "all" — **παντὶ** (*panti*): each and every part; all inclusive; no one excluded or missing

4. "hath made" — **τίθημι** (*tithemi*): to set in place; to position; to fix; to establish

5. "overseers" — **ἐπίσκοπος** (*episkopos*): to look over; oversight; to administrate or manage; a supervisory position; one whose responsibility is to guide, direct, and give oversight; to serve as a bishop

6. "feed" — **ποιμαίνω** (*poimaino*): to shepherd; to tend; to rule; to govern; pictures feeding, guarding, guiding, and protecting a flock

7. "church" — **ἐκκλησία** (*ekklesia*): a called, separated, and prestigious assembly; a prestigious assembly of distinguished citizens who determined laws, debated public policy, formulated new policies, argued and ruled in judicial matters, elected the chief magistrates of the land, and decided who should be banished; to be selected from society and invited to join this assembly was a great honor; in the New Testament, it depicts the body of believers who have been called out, called forth, selected, and assembled to be God's representatives in every town, city, state or nation; a body called to make decisions that affect the atmosphere of a region

8. "purchased" — **περιποιέω** (*peripoieo*): pictures a comprehensive purchase; total purchase; completely purchased and taken wholly

9. "elders" — **πρεσβύτερος** (*presbuteros*): depicts the spiritual representatives of Israel, such as ruling members of local synagogues or teachers of the Law who publicly taught in synagogues; such elders were deemed worthy of honor due to their positions; pictures those who have legal or spiritual authority; officially appointed church leaders

10. "exhort" — **παρακαλέω** (*parakaleo*): to encourage; to exhort; to console someone else; to encourage and stir troops to attentiveness and action; to pray or beg; an appeal intended to ignite a hearer to action

11. "taking the oversight" — **ἐπίσκοπος** (*episkopos*): to look over; oversight; to administrate or manage; a supervisory position; one whose responsibility is to guide, direct, and give oversight; to serve as a bishop

12. "constraint" — **ἀναγκαστῶς** (*anagkastos*): compulsion; by force; against one's will

13. "willingly" — **ἑκουσίως** (*hekousios*): willingly; of one's free will; of one's own accord

14. "according to God" — **κατὰ Θεόν** (*kata Theon*): being answerable to God

15. "filthy lucre" — **αἰσχροκερδῶς** (*aischrokerdos*): shameful gain; for a dirty game of cards; shamefully throwing dice to make a gain; imply-

ing that the task is more than a game
to be played for financial gain

16. "ready mind" — προθύμως (*prothumos*): enthusiastically willing; eager; ready to do

17. "ensamples" — τύπος (*tupos*): an example; a permanent impression; a copy; an image; a pattern; a model for others to follow; a pattern for others to see and imitate

18. "chief Shepherd" — ἀρχιποίμην (*archipoimen*): the chief shepherd; the head shepherd; the arch-shepherd

SYNOPSIS

Shepherds have played a valuable role in the culture of the nation of Israel since its inception. The ancient ruins in the mountains just outside the city of Bethlehem reveal that it was a place where shepherds regularly kept watch over their flocks.

In many ways, pastors are like spiritual shepherds to their congregations, and this comparative imagery is used throughout Scripture. Their primary responsibility is to provide spiritual nourishment for the sheep. Additionally, they are to faithfully oversee all that goes on in the local church and be faithful to the Holy Spirit's calling on their lives.

The emphasis of this lesson:

Pastors are selected by the Holy Spirit to oversee the most prestigious people on the planet — the Church. They are called to feed and care for God's sheep and be a shining example of Christ that they can imitate.

A Quick Review of What We Learned About Pastors

In our last lesson, we took a close look at God's reprimand of the shepherds of Israel in Ezekiel 34. By reading through God's point-by-point rebuke of the things they were failing to do, we can determine what a shepherd — or pastor — is supposed to do. For a detailed list of these pastoral duties, please refer to Lesson 7.

We also looked at John 10:11 in which Jesus said, "I am the good shepherd: the good shepherd giveth his life for the sheep." In Greek, the phrase "the good shepherd" is *ho poimen ho kalos*. The words *ho poimen* refer to *the shepherd — the feeder, the protector, and the ruler of a flock of men* or *a local congregation*. The words *ho kalos* — translated here as "good" — refer to *the good one, the most excellent one,* or *the one who is the supreme example.* Hence, when Jesus said, "I am the Good Shepherd," He was saying, "I am the supreme example of what a spiritual shepherd (a pastor) should be. There is no better shepherd than Me."

Every pastor would be wise to look carefully at the life of Jesus and model their pastoral ministry after His. Although there is no such thing as a perfect pastor, most pastors really try their best to represent Christ as best as they can.

We concluded our previous lesson by quickly noting *seven specific duties of a good pastor.*

A good pastor knows...

1. The state of his sheep (or congregation).
2. How to nourish, feed, and reprove the sheep to bring them into a state of spiritual soundness.
3. How to rescue and restore the sheep that have fallen into sin.
4. How to find the sheep that have been driven away. Inevitably, believers sometimes don't understand why something happened and they become offended with someone in the church and leave. A good pastor knows how to find those who have left the fellowship.
5. How to bring sheep that have strayed into strange pastures back into the fold. Sometimes believers get off into strange teaching, and a pastor has the responsibility to bring them back into the fold.
6. How to oppose and expel wolves that have gotten in among the sheep, scattering them from each other and from God.
7. How to preach, explain, and defend the truth for the sheep.

The Holy Spirit Handpicks Each Pastor

In Acts 20:28, the apostle Paul spoke to the elders, or pastors, of the Church of Ephesus and said, "Take heed therefore unto yourselves, and to all the flock, over the which the Holy Ghost hath made you overseers, to feed the church of God, which he hath purchased with his own blood." Here again we see the primary responsibility of pastors is *to feed the people of God.*

But also notice the words "take heed." It is the Greek word *prosecho*, which means *giving one's full attention to what is being spoken and heard and drawing as near to it as possible*. It depicts *a person giving his or her full attention to a matter*. It can also mean *to apply the mind to a thing* or *to give serious consideration and contemplation to what is being heard*. Thus, when Paul said, "'take heed,'" he didn't just ask the pastors in Ephesus to *listen*. He urged them to give their entire attention to what he was saying and take it seriously.

He then added the words, "to all the flock." The word "all" is the Greek word *panti*, which means *each and every part*. It is all-inclusive; no one excluded or missing. In other words, the pastor is responsible for *every person* who is a member of the church (or flock) — not just the ones he likes.

Paul went on to tell the pastors they were to care for "all the flock, over the which the Holy Ghost hath made you overseers..." (Acts 20:28). The phrase "hath made" is a translation of the Greek word *tithemi*, which means *to set in place*; *to position*; or *to fix*; *to establish*. A pastor is one who has been set in place and fixed in position by the Holy Spirit; they are not self-appointed. As such, they are accountable to the Holy Spirit for the way they carry out their pastoral responsibilities as "overseers."

The word "overseers" is the Greek word *episkopos*, and it means *to look over, to have oversight, to administrate*, or *to manage*. It describes *a supervisory position; one whose responsibility is to guide, direct, and give oversight*. Moreover, it is the word that means *to serve as a bishop*. Again, it is the Holy Spirit that chooses the individuals He desires to serve as supervisors, managers, and administrators of the local churches.

Pastors Are Privileged To Oversee the Most Prestigious People on the Planet

Paul said that their primary responsibility is to "to feed the church of God...." The word "feed" is the Greek word *poimaino*, which means *to shepherd, to tend, to rule,* or *to govern*. It pictures *feeding, guarding, guiding, and protecting a flock*. In this case, the "flock" is the "church of God." The word for "church" is the Greek word *ekklesia*. It is a compound of the word *ek*, which means *out*, and the word *klesia*, from the word *kaleo*, meaning *to call*. When the two words are compounded, they form the word *ekklesia* or "church."

This word was not originally found in Scripture but was borrowed from the Athenian culture. It described *a called, separated, and prestigious assembly; a prestigious assembly of distinguished citizens who determined laws, debated public policy, formulated new policies, argued and ruled in judicial matters, elected the chief magistrates of the land, and decided who should be banished.* To be selected from society and invited to join this assembly was a great honor.

In the New Testament, it depicts *the body of believers who have been called out, called forth, selected, and assembled to be God's representatives in every town, city, state or nation; a body called to make decisions that affect the atmosphere of the region in which they lived.* Furthermore, these *called out ones* (the Church) have been "…purchased with his own blood" (Acts 20:28). The word "purchased" is from the Greek word *peripoieo*, and it pictures *a comprehensive or total purchase; completely purchased and taken wholly.*

The point in all this is that when pastors grow weary and become frustrated working with people, they must remember that it is an honor to be a pastor. They have been uniquely selected by the Holy Spirit to oversee — manage, supervise, and administrate — the Church. And the Church is not just any group of people. It is the most prestigious group of individuals on the face of the earth. They have been *wholly* purchased with the blood of Jesus and called out by God to make decisions that affect the atmosphere of the regions in which they live.

Peter Exhorted Pastors To Feed and To Oversee God's People

Peter was a pastor in the Early Church, and in First Peter 5:1, he spoke specifically to his fellow pastors and said, "The elders which are among you I exhort, who am also an elder, and a witness of the sufferings of Christ, and also a partaker of the glory that shall be revealed."

Notice that Peter called himself an "elder" — the Greek word *presbuteros*. It is from where we get the word *Presbyterian*, and it depicts *the spiritual representatives of Israel, such as ruling members of local synagogues or teachers of the Law who publicly taught in synagogues.* Such elders were deemed worthy of honor due to their God-given positions. The word *presbuteros* also pictures *those who have legal or spiritual authority* or *have been officially appointed church leaders.* This is what Peter said he was and who he was addressing in First Peter 5 — the "elders" (*presbuteros*).

Specifically, Peter took time to "exhort" the other elders among him. The word "exhort" is the Greek word *parakaleo*, and it means *to encourage, to exhort*, or *to console someone else*. In a military sense, it meant *to encourage and stir troops to attentiveness and action*. It can also mean *to pray* or *to beg*; *it is an appeal intended to ignite a hearer to action*.

What was Peter exhorting his fellow pastors to do? He said, "Feed the flock of God which is among you..." (1 Peter 5:2). Here again we see the word "feed" — the Greek word *poimaino*, meaning *to shepherd, to tend, to rule*, or *to govern*. It pictures *feeding, guarding, guiding, and protecting a flock, or local congregation*.

Peter said, "Feed the flock of God which is among you, taking the oversight thereof..." (1 Peter 5:2). The word "oversight" is once again the Greek word *episkopos*, which means *to look over, to administrate*, or *to manage*. It describes *one in a supervisory position whose responsibility is to guide, direct, and give oversight to the local congregation*.

This spiritual guide is not perfect, but to the best of his ability, he is to take "...the oversight thereof, not by constraint, but willingly [according to God]..." (1 Peter 5:2). The word "constraint" is the Greek word *anagkastos*, and in this case it means *not by compulsion* or *by force* or *against one's will*. Rather, he is to lead "willingly." This is the Greek word *hekousios*, which means *willingly, of one's free will*, or *of one's own accord*.

What is interesting here is that when you read this portion of Scripture in the original Greek, it includes the phrase "according to God" immediately after the word "willingly." The implication here is that every pastor is going to be *accountable to God* regarding his pastoral duties. Again, these spiritual leaders didn't appoint themselves; they were appointed by God, and therefore will be answerable to Him.

Pastoral Ministry Should Never Be About Money

Peter went on to say that elders, or spiritual overseers, were to serve "...not for filthy lucre, but of a ready mind" (1 Peter 5:2). The word "filthy lucre" is the Greek word *aischrokerdos*, and it describes *shameful gain; a dirty game of cards*; or *shamefully throwing dice to make a gain*. It implies that *the task is more than a game to be played for financial gain*.

In other words, when a person is called to pastoral ministry, it is not so that he can make an exorbitant salary. If wealth is the aim, the person is in the wrong position. Although receiving a large salary in and of itself is not wrong and each flock should generously take care of its shepherd, big money should never be the ambition of a pastor or anyone else serving in ministry.

Jesus is the Good Shepherd, and as our example, He laid down His life for us, His sheep (*see* John 10:11). The only profit He looked forward to receiving through His obedience was knowing that He pleased the father by fulfilling His will (*see* Jon 17:4) and seeing people who would believe on Him as the Son of God and Savior of the world in Heaven. Pastoral ministry is all about *giving*, not getting.

Instead of filthy lucre being the motivator, Peter said it should be "a ready mind." The words "ready mind" is the Greek word *prothumos*, and it means *to be enthusiastically willing or eager, ready to do*. The role of a pastor is an assignment given by Heaven. Thus, it is a privilege to serve God's people as a shepherd (*poimen*), an overseer (*episkopos*), or an elder (*presbuteros*). Pastoral ministry is one of great influence, and those called by God to serve in this capacity should be eager and enthusiastic about it.

Pastors Are Examples for Others To Imitate

Peter went on to say, "Neither as being lords over God's heritage, but being ensamples to the flock" (1 Peter 5:3). The word "ensamples" is a translation of the Greek word *tupos*, and it describes *an example; a permanent impression; a copy; an image; a pattern; a model for others to follow; a pattern for others to see and imitate*.

Without question, if you are a pastor, people are watching your life closely. They watch the way you teach, the way you worship, and the way you pray. In fact, everything you do becomes a sermon — from the way you treat your spouse and take care of your home, to the way you use your finances and the entertainment you choose. It is as if you are living in a glass fishbowl with observers all around, listening to what you say and watching what you do.

At this point it must be said that there are no perfect pastors. So if you are looking for one, give up your search. Just as there are no perfect sheep, neither is there a perfect pastor. All of us are imperfect human beings. The only One who is perfect is Jesus. That is why He said, "I am the good shepherd — I am the supreme example above all others of what a pastor should be."

To the pastors who take their calling seriously and give themselves to executing it with excellence, Peter said, "When the chief Shepherd shall appear, ye shall receive a crown of glory that fadeth not away" (1 Peter 5:4). The phrase "chief Shepherd" in Greek is *archipoimen*, and it means *the chief shepherd, the head shepherd*, or *the arch-shepherd*. One day the Chief Shepherd is going to return to earth, and when He does, He is going to give a special crown to pastors who have carried out their jobs faithfully.

STUDY QUESTIONS

> Study to shew thyself approved unto God, a workman that needeth
> not to be ashamed, rightly dividing the word of truth.
> — 2 Timothy 2:15

1. Acts 20:28 says the Holy Spirit selects those who are to serve in pastoral ministry, and He plants each pastor where He chooses. According to First Corinthians 12:18, who should determine where you are to be placed in the Body of Christ (the church where you attend and serve)?

2. When God looks at you, He sees you as *righteous* in Christ (*see* 2 Corinthians 5:21). According to Psalm 92:12-15, what can you expect to see happening in and through your life, all throughout your life? Where must you remain in order to experience these wonderful things take place (*see* verse 13)?

3. Take a few moments to reflect on the definition of the word "church" — the Greek word *ekklesia*. How does the meaning of this word humble and challenge you as a servant of God?

PRACTICAL APPLICATION

> But be ye doers of the word, and not hearers only,
> deceiving your own selves.
> — James 1:22

Galatians 6:10 (*AMPC*) says, "…Be mindful to be a blessing, especially to those of the household of faith [those who belong to God's family with you, the believers]. Stop and think. *Is my mind full of ways to be a blessing to those of the household of faith — including my pastor?* Here a couple of ideas to help get you started.

1. What do you appreciate most about your pastor? How about the associate pastor(s)?

2. When was the last time you sent them a quick handwritten note of thanks? Why not take a little time this week and write out a *thank you* note for your pastor. And while you're at it, attach a gift card to one of his favorite places to eat or shop. Remember, what you plant you will reap, and as you refresh others, you too will be refreshed (*see* Galatians 6:7; Proverbs 11:25).

3. Another wonderful way to bless your pastor and his family is by *praying* for them. First Timothy 2:1-3 says you are to pray for those in authority, which includes your pastor. Take time now to ask God to pour out His blessings of wisdom, peace, provision, protection, favor, boldness, direction, and joy on your pastor and his family. Bless his marriage and relationships with unity and peace, and pray that strife and division would be bound. Bless His personal relationship with Jesus with fresh revelation of truth and the anointing of the Holy Spirit.

LESSON 9

TOPIC

The Ministry of the Teacher, Part 1

SCRIPTURES

1. **Ephesians 4:11** — And he gave some, apostles; and some, prophets; and some, evangelists; and some, pastors and teachers.

2. **Matthew 8:19** — And a certain scribe came, and said unto him, Master, I will follow thee whithersoever thou goest.

3. **Matthew 9:11** — And when the Pharisees saw it, they said unto his disciples, Why eateth your Master with publicans and sinners?

4. **Matthew 19:16** — And, behold, one came and said unto him, Good Master, what good thing shall I do, that I may have eternal life?

5. **Matthew 26:25** — Then Judas, which betrayed him, answered and said, Master, is it I? He said unto him, Thou hast said.

6. **Matthew 26:49** — And forthwith he [Judas] came to Jesus, and said, Hail, Master; and kissed him.

7. **Mark 9:5** — And Peter answered and said to Jesus, Master, it is good for us to be here: and let us make three tabernacles; one for thee, and one for Moses, and one for Elias.

8. **Mark 11:21** — And Peter calling to remembrance saith unto him, Master, behold, the fig tree which thou cursedst is withered away.

9. **Mark 13:1** — And as he went out of the temple, one of his disciples saith unto him, Master, see what manner of stones and what buildings are here!

10. **Mark 14:45** — And as soon as he was come, he goeth straightway to him, and saith, Master, master; and kissed him.

11. **Luke 10:25** — And, behold, a certain lawyer stood up, and tempted him, saying, Master, what shall I do to inherit eternal life?

12. **Luke 19:39** — And some of the Pharisees from among the multitude said unto him, Master, rebuke thy disciples.

13. **Luke 20:21** — And they asked him, saying, Master (διδάσκαλος), we know that thou sayest and teachest rightly, neither acceptest thou the person of any, but teachest the way of God truly.

14. **Luke 20:39** — Then certain of the scribes answering said, Master, thou hast well said.

15. **Luke 21:7** — And they asked him, saying, Master, but when shall these things be? and what sign will there be when these things shall come to pass?"

16. **John 1:38** — Then Jesus turned, and saw them following, and saith unto them, What seek ye? They said unto him, Rabbi, (which is to say, being interpreted, Master,) where dwellest thou?

17. **John 1:49** — Nathanael answered and saith unto him, Rabbi, thou art the Son of God; thou art the King of Israel.

18. **John 3:2** — The same came to Jesus by night, and said unto him, Rabbi, we know that thou art a Teacher come from God: for no man can do these miracles that thou doest, except God be with him.

19. **John 4:31** — In the mean while his disciples prayed him, saying, Master, eat.

20. **John 6:25** — And when they had found him on the other side of the sea, they said unto him, Rabbi, when camest thou hither?

21. **John 11:8** — His disciples say unto him, Master, the Jews of late sought to stone thee; and goest thou thither again?

22. **John 13:13** — Ye call me Master and Lord: and ye say well; for so I am.

23. **John 20:16** — Jesus saith unto her, Mary. She turned herself, and saith unto him, Rabboni; which is to say, Master.

24. **Mark 3:14** — that they might be with him.

GREEK WORDS

1. "teacher" — **διδάσκαλος** (*didaskalos*): a teacher; one who is a fabulous, masterful teacher; the Greek equivalent for the Hebrew word rabbi; the word **διδάσκαλος** (*didaskalos*) is used 47 times in the gospels; it is derived from **διδάσκω** (*didasko*), which means to teach, to instruct, or to prescribe; primarily described the relationship between a teacher and a pupil or between a master and an apprentice; the word "teacher" — *didaskalos* — is often translated "master"

2. "Rabbi" — ʹ**Ραββί** (*rhabbi*): rabbi; a teacher-scholar who was respected for his accumulation of facts and knowledge; literally means "great in number"; refers to the great number of facts and knowledge possessed by a rabbi; used interchangeably with "teacher," **διδάσκαλος** (*didaskalos*)

3. "disciple" — **μαθητής** (*mathetes*): pupil; student; learner

SYNOPSIS

The ancient city of Magdala is located on the western shore of the Sea of Galilee, in the region of Galilee. It is the place from where Mary Magdalene hailed. In this city today there is a well-preserved synagogue from the First Century that has been recently excavated, and it is probably the same synagogue in which Jesus Himself stood and taught as a rabbi.

Teachers are one of the fivefold gifts Jesus gave to the Church. Ephesians 4:11 says, "And he gave some, apostles; and some, prophets; and some, evangelists; and some, pastors and teachers." Just as Jesus functioned in the role of Apostle, Prophet, Evangelist, and Pastor, He was also a Masterful Teacher — One who spoke with great authority and had a masterful grip of the Scriptures.

The emphasis of this lesson:

A teacher is one who has a masterful grip on the Scriptures, a wealth of knowledge, and speaks with authority. The words *teacher*, *master*, and

rabbi are used interchangeably throughout the New Testament. All three essentially mean the same thing.

What Does the Word 'Teacher' Mean?

The word "teacher" is the Greek word *didaskalos*, and it is the word primarily translated as "teacher" in the New Testament. It describes *a teacher, one who is a fabulous, masterful teacher*. It is the Greek equivalent of the Hebrew word for *rabbi*. It is derived from the Greek word *didasko*, which means *to teach, instruct*, or *to prescribe*. This word primarily described the relationship between a teacher and a pupil, or between a master and an apprentice.

The word *didaskalos* is used 47 times in the gospels. The Greek word *didasko*, which forms the foundation of the word *didaskalos*, is used more than 200 times in the Old Testament Greek Septuagint and in the Greek New Testament. Any word that is used with such frequency is a very well-established word with a clearly defined meaning. Again, it means *to teach, to inform, to instruct, to demonstrate*, or *to prescribe*, and *it depicts the relationship between a teacher and a pupil*, or *an instructor and an apprentice*.

The word *didaskolos* pictures the learning of a student at the side of his teacher, who's ever at his side. In history, such teachers would sit right by their students to instruct them, and it was the student's responsibility to listen, to obey, to internalize, and to put into practice the truths that they were learning from their teacher. Thus, a *didaskolos* is one who has authority to speak into the lives of his students.

The word *didaskolos* is so powerful and carries such authority that in the New Testament it is often translated as the word "master." Even in today's educational system, scholars are often referred to as "masters." If you go to a university and you want a higher level of education, the first level of education you receive is called a "master's" degree. The word "master" carries the idea of *one with great information — someone that is well-instructed and possesses a wealth of knowledge*.

The word "rabbi" is also significant, as it describes *a teacher-scholar who was respected for his accumulation of facts and knowledge*. The word "rabbi" literally means *great in number*, and this refers to the great number of facts and knowledge that a rabbi possesses. Given their meanings, the words *teacher*, *master*, and *rabbi* are used interchangeably all throughout the New Testament. All three essentially mean the same thing.

Examples of Teachers in the New Testament

There are several examples of teachers in the New Testament. In Acts 13:1, we see the elders of the Church of Antioch gathered together seeking the Lord in prayer and fasting. Two of them were teachers. One was named *Manaen* and the other one was *Saul*, who later came to be called Paul.

In Acts 18:24 and 25, we find a certain Jew by the name of *Apollos* who was "an eloquent man, and mighty in the scriptures." The Greek word here for "eloquent" means he was very educated and well-versed. History reveals that Apollos was not only a masterful teacher, but he also went on to become the leader of the Church in Corinth for a time. In fact, Early Church fathers wrote that Apollos was a golden-tongued orator through whom the Scripture freely flowed. He knew so much Scripture that some scholars speculate he may have been the one that wrote the book of Hebrews.

In Acts 18:26, we see two more masterful teachers — Aquila and Priscilla. Interestingly, most scholars believe that Priscilla had the greater teaching gift of the two of them. At that time, they were in the city of Ephesus and heard Apollos teaching eloquently and mightily in the town's synagogue. But since Apollos only knew and taught about the baptism of John, they took him aside and "expounded unto him the way of God more perfectly." Thus, Aquila and Priscilla were teachers.

Then, of course, we know that Paul was a teacher. In First Timothy 2:7, he said, "Whereunto I am ordained a preacher, and an apostle (I speak the truth in Christ, and lie not;) a *teacher* of the Gentiles in faith and verity." Indeed, the apostle Paul would become one of the greatest teachers of Scripture the world will ever know — both orally and through his written letters, which later became books of the New Testament.

As we noted in the introduction, Jesus not only functioned in the role of apostle, prophet, evangelist, and pastor, He also was a Masterful Teacher — the Greek word *didaskalos*. He spoke with great authority and had a masterful grip of the Scriptures. Let's look at a sampling of passages from the gospels in which Jesus is referred to as "Teacher," "Master," and "Rabbi."

'Teacher,' 'Master,' and 'Rabbi'
Are Interchangeable Terms

Matthew 8:19 — "And a certain scribe came, and said unto him, Master, I will follow thee whithersoever thou goest." The word "master" is the Greek word *didaskalos*, meaning *masterful teacher*. When people called Jesus *didaskalos*, they were recognizing Him as *One that had a mastery of knowledge*.

Matthew 9:11 — "And when the Pharisees saw it, they said unto his disciples, Why eateth your Master with publicans and sinners?" Here we see the Pharisees actually recognizing Jesus' authority. That's why they called Him a "Master" — the Greek *didaskalos*, meaning *masterful teacher*.

Matthew 19:16 — "And, behold, one came and said unto him, Good Master, what good thing shall I do, that I may have eternal life?" In this verse, when the rich young ruler called Jesus "Master," he used the word *didaskalos*, meaning *masterful teacher, the One who is superior in knowledge and masterful of facts and information*.

Matthew 26:25 — "Then Judas, which betrayed him, answered and said, Master, is it I? He said unto him, Thou hast said." Interestingly, when Judas addressed Jesus as "Master" here, he used the Greek word *rhabbi*, not *didaskalos*. The translators rendered it as "Master" in the *King James Version*.

Matthew 26:49 — "And forthwith he [Judas] came to Jesus, and said, Hail, Master; and kissed him." Here again, Judas called Jesus "Master," which is often a translation of the Greek word *didaskalos*, but in this case it is *rabbi*. This demonstrates how the words "teacher" and "master" are used interchangeably.

Mark 9:5 — "And Peter answered and said to Jesus, Master, it is good for us to be here: and let us make three tabernacles; one for thee, and one for Moses, and one for Elias." In this verse, Peter, James, and John were with Jesus on the Mount of Transfiguration, and Peter called Him *rabbi*, but it is translated as "Master."

Mark 11:21 — "And Peter calling to remembrance saith unto him, Master, behold, the fig tree which thou cursedst is withered away." Here again, the word "Master" is the Greek word *rhabbi*, not *didaskalos*.

Mark 13:1 — "And as he went out of the temple, one of his disciples saith unto him, Master, see what manner of stones and what buildings are here!" In this verse, the disciples called Jesus "Master," and it is the Greek word *didaskalos*. Again, this shows the interchangeableness of the words "teacher" and "master."

Mark 14:45 — "And as soon as he was come, he goeth straightway to him, and saith, Master, master; and kissed him." Here, Jesus was in the Garden of Gethsemane, and when Judas entered and approached Him, he said, "*Rhabbi, rhabbi*," in Greek, yet it is translated as, "Master, master!"

Luke 10:25 — "And, behold, a certain lawyer stood up, and tempted him, saying, Master, what shall I do to inherit eternal life?" The word "Master" here is the Greek word *didaskalos*, meaning *supreme teacher, masterful teacher*.

Luke 19:39 — "And some of the Pharisees from among the multitude said unto him, Master, rebuke thy disciples." In this verse, just as in Matthew 9:11, the Pharisees called Jesus "Master" — the Greek word *didaskalos* — which means they were recognizing Jesus' authority and His mastery of the Scriptures.

Luke 20:21 — "And they asked him, saying, Master, we know that thou sayest and teachest rightly, neither acceptest thou the person of any, but teachest the way of God truly." In this verse, spies had been sent by the Pharisees to trip up and trap Jesus. Interestingly, they called Him "Master," which in this case is the Greek word *didaskalos*. This means they were recognizing Jesus' masterful handling of the Scriptures.

Luke 20:39 — "Then certain of the scribes answering said, Master, thou hast well said." Here again, the word "Master" is the Greek word *didaskalos*, which means the scribes were recognizing Jesus astute handling of the Scriptures as a masterful teacher.

Luke 21:7 — "And they asked him, saying, Master, but when shall these things be? and what sign will there be when these things shall come to pass?" Here, the disciples were asking Jesus about the end of the age and His return, and they called Him "Master," the Greek word *didaskalos*, meaning *masterful teacher*. They were recognizing His supreme authority regarding the Word of God.

John 1:38 — "Then Jesus turned, and saw them following, and saith unto them, What seek ye? They said unto him, Rabbi, (which is to say, being interpreted, Master,) where dwellest thou?" In this verse we find both words. First, they called Jesus "Rabbi," which is the Greek word *rhabbi*, meaning *a teacher-scholar who was respected for his accumulation of facts and knowledge*. Then it says, "...being interpreted, Master," which is the Greek word *didaskalos*. So, this verse emphatically demonstrates that the word *rhabbi* and the word *didaskalos* have the very same meaning.

John 1:49 — "Nathanael answered and saith unto him, Rabbi, thou art the Son of God; thou art the King of Israel." Here it is just translated as the word "Rabbi," but it means *masterful teacher*.

John 3:2 — "The same came to Jesus by night, and said unto him, Rabbi, we know that thou art a teacher come from God: for no man can do these miracles that thou doest, except God be with him." In this verse, Nicodemus came to Jesus under cover of night wanting to know more about Him, and he addressed Jesus as both "Rabbi" and "teacher" — the Greek words *rhabbi* and *didaskalos* respectively.

John 4:31 — "In the mean while his disciples prayed him, saying, Master, eat." The word translated "Master" here is the Greek word *rhabbi*.

John 6:25 — "And when they had found him on the other side of the sea, they said unto him, Rabbi, when camest thou hither?" Here again, the word "Rabbi" is the Greek word *rhabbi*, meaning *masterful teacher; one who is supreme when it comes to handling the Scriptures*.

John 11:8 — "His disciples say unto him, Master, the Jews of late sought to stone thee; and goest thou thither again?" Just before returning to Judea to raise Lazarus from the dead, the disciples questioned Jesus, calling Him "Master," and in this case it is the Greek word *rhabbi*, not *didaskalos*.

John 13:13 — "Ye call me Master and Lord: and ye say well; for so I am." The word translated "Master" here in the *King James Version* is the Greek word *didaskalos*, which is the word for *masterful teacher*. Once more, this shows how the words "teacher" and "master" are used interchangeably.

Also notice Jesus said, "Ye call me Master and *Lord*..." This is very important because if you were a *didaksalos* (teacher) or a *rhabbi* (rabbi), you were also considered a "lord." That is, you had great authority over your students. In essence, Jesus said, "When you call Me *didaskalos* (teacher), you're acknowledging that I have authority to speak into your life. And as My students, you are supposed to listen to Me, internalize what I say, and do what I instruct you to do. I'm your Master, your Teacher, and your Rabbi. I have scriptural and spiritual authority."

John 20:16 — "Jesus saith unto her, Mary. She turned herself, and saith unto him, Rabboni; which is to say, Master." Here Jesus was confronted by Mary Magdalene in the garden just after His resurrection. She called Him "Rabboni," which is the Greek word *rhabbi*, meaning *great one*. Then the Bible immediately clarifies "...which is to say, Master." The word "Master" is the Greek word, *didaskalos*, meaning *masterful teacher*. Again, both words are used side-by-side in the same verse, demonstrating their equality.

The point and purpose for going through all these verses is to help you see and understand the interchangeableness of these words in the New Testament. Again and again and again, the word "teacher," the Greek word *didaskalos*, is interchanged with the word "rabbi," the Greek word *rhabbi*. All of these words used together describe an *outstanding, masterful, great teacher*. And while these words clearly describe Jesus, they are also used interchangeably to describe those that operate in the fivefold ministry gift of *teacher*.

Students and Teachers Share an Intimately Close Relationship

There is something else important to understand about *rabbis* and *teachers*, and that is every one of them had students. In the time of the New Testament, there were no seminaries. So, *rabbis* would gather a group of students around themselves and take them everywhere they went.

Students would listen to him, follow him, and imitate his life and lifestyle. Virtually every moment they were together became a teaching moment.

Each student or apprentice would submit to his teacher or master, and there was a close relationship between them. The teacher had the right to speak into the lives of his pupils. The pupil's job was to hear his teacher, internalize what he said, and put it into practice. The student or apprentice was also to help his teacher or master with his ministry or business. They weren't just listeners.

This brings us to the word "disciples." It is the Greek word *methetes*, and it describes *a pupil, a student,* or *a learner.* Jesus' twelve "disciples" were actually the twelve *learners.* That is a literal translation of the word. In Mark 3:14, it says Jesus, "…ordained twelve, that they should be with him, and that he might send them forth to preach." This verse describes the relationship between a teacher and his pupils — between a master and his apprentices. Just like the word *didaskalos* describes a teacher who would sit and stay at the side of his pupil and teach him, the disciples were chosen to be with Jesus, and He was literally at their side teaching them. They were able to learn because Jesus spoke into their lives with authority, and they recognized Him as *Teacher, Master,* and *Rabbi.*

All of this is foundational to understanding the fivefold ministry gift of a teacher. A teacher is not just someone who opens their Bible and explains a few verses. A real, Christ-appointed teacher is a *rhabbi* or a *didaskalos.* They have a masterful grip of the Scriptures and speak with great authority.

If you have a relationship with a God-given teacher — if you are his or her disciple — it means you are in subjection to them, and they have the right to speak direction into your life. Your role is to listen, to obey, to internalize, and put what they say to you into practice.

STUDY QUESTIONS

Study to shew thyself approved unto God, a workman that needeth not to be ashamed, rightly dividing the word of truth.
— 2 Timothy 2:15

1. What new insights did you gain about a "teacher" from the meaning of the word *didaskalos*? How about from the words "rabbi" and "master"?

2. In many ways the relationship between a "teacher" (*didaskalos*) and his student resembles the relationship between a "rabbi" (*rhabbi*) and his "disciple" (*mathetes*). What similarities can you identify?

3. In your own words, tell how you can know for sure that someone is a genuine, Christ-given, fivefold ministry teacher.

PRACTICAL APPLICATION

> But be ye doers of the word, and not hearers only,
> deceiving your own selves.
> — James 1:22

Who would you say has functioned — or is functioning — as a "teacher" or "rabbi" in your life? What are some of the most life-changing principles and truths they have taught you? Do you value what they have taught you, and have you taken the time to personally express your thanks for taking the time to invest in your life?

1. In New Testament times, *rabbis* would gather a group of students around themselves and take them everywhere they went. A student's job was to listen to him, follow him, and imitate his life and lifestyle. The pupil was also to be in subjection to his teacher, giving him the right to speak direction into his life. Are you doing your part as a student? In what areas could you come up higher?

LESSON 10

TOPIC

The Ministry of the Teacher, Part 2

SCRIPTURES

1. **Ephesians 4:11** — And he gave some, apostles; and some, prophets; and some, evangelists; and some, pastors and teachers.

2. **James 3:1** — My brethren, be not many masters, knowing that we shall receive the greater condemnation.

3. **1 Timothy 1:7** — Desiring to be teachers of the law; understanding neither what they say, nor whereof they affirm

4. **Ezra 7:6** (*NLT*) — This Ezra was a scribe, [who] was well versed in the law...

5. **Ezra 7:6** (*NKJV*) — ...he was a skilled scribe in the law ...

6. **Nehemiah 8:8** (*NIV*) — They read from the Book of the Law of God, making it clear and giving the meaning so that the people could understand what was being read.

7. **Nehemiah 8:8** (*NLT*) — They read from the Book of the Law of God and clearly explained the meaning of what was being read, helping the people understand each passage.

8. **Nehemiah 8:8** (*NASB*) — They read from the book, from the law of God, translating to give the sense so that they understood the reading.

9. **Nehemiah 8:8** (*NKJV*) — So they read distinctly from the book, in the Law of God; and they gave the sense, and helped them to understand the reading.

GREEK WORDS

1. "teacher" — **διδάσκαλος** (*didaskalos*): a teacher; one who is a fabulous, masterful teacher; the Greek equivalent of the Hebrew word for rabbi; the word **διδάσκαλος** (*didaskalos*) is used 47 times in the gospels; it is derived from **διδάσκω** (*didasko*), which means to teach, to instruct, or to prescribe; primarily described the relationship between a teacher and a pupil or between a master and an apprentice; the word "teacher" — *didaskalos* — is often translated "master."

2. "many" — **πολλοί** (*polloi*): a great number

3. "masters" — **διδάσκαλος** (*didaskalos*): a teacher; one who is a fabulous, masterful teacher; the Greek equivalent of the Hebrew word for rabbi

4. "greater" — **μεῖζόν** (*meidzon*): far greater by comparison

5. "condemnation" — **κρίμα** (*krima*): a verdict or judgment that results from a formal investigation

6. "desiring" — **θέλω** (*thelo*): to earnestly desire; to long for; depicts an earnest, ongoing desire

7. "teachers of the law" — **νομοδιδάσκαλος** (*nomodidaskalos*): a compound of **νόμος** (*nomos*) and **διδάσκαλος** (*didaskalos*); the word **νόμος** (*nomos*) means rules, principles, or the unchanging and unbendable rule of faith; **διδάσκαλος** (*didaskalos*) refers to a masterful teacher; compounded, **νομοδιδάσκαλος** (*nomodidaskalos*) pictures a masterful scripture-lawyer; someone scholarly in interpreting the Bible

8. "understanding" — **νοοῦντες** (*noountes*): a derivative of the word **νοῦς** (*nous*); to perceive; refers to the mind and the ability to think, reason, understand, and comprehend; not comprehending

9. "affirm" — **διαβεβαιόομαι** (*diabebaioomai*): continuous sense, to continuously assert; to continuously establish or affirm confidently

SYNOPSIS

Not long ago, a synagogue dating back to the First Century was excavated in the city of Magdala. This Galilean city was the home of Mary Magdalene and a place where Jesus frequently taught. Of all the teachers, He was the most Masterful Teacher — the Rabbi above all rabbis. When He opened His mouth, He opened the Old Testament scriptures like no one else could.

After His ministry on earth was complete and He ascended into Heaven, He took of the anointing that was on His life and released it to the Church in the form of the fivefold ministry gifts. Ephesians 4:11 emphatically declares, "And he gave some, apostles; and some, prophets; and some, evangelists; and some, pastors and teachers." All these gifts that were in full operation in Christ's life are alive and well in the world today — including the gift of teaching!

The emphasis of this lesson:

A New Testament teacher is one who is firmly grounded in Scripture and speaks with authority into the lives of his students. Due to his position of great influence, his life will be scrutinized by God Himself and held to a higher standard. It is a serious responsibility one should not take lightly.

A Quick Review of What
We Know About a Teacher

As we saw in our last lesson, the word "teacher" in Greek is the word *didaskalos*. It is the primary word used for "teacher" in the New Testament. This word *didaskalos* describes *a teacher* or *one who is a fabulous, masterful teacher*. It is the Greek equivalent of the Hebrew word for *rabbi*. The word *didaksalos* is used 47 times in the gospels, and it is derived from the Greek word *didasko*, which means *to teach, instruct,* or *to prescribe*. The word *didasko*, which forms the word for *didaskalos*, is used more than 200 times in the Old Testament Greek Septuagint and in the Greek New Testament. Thus, we really know what this word means.

What is interesting is that the word *didaskalos* primarily described the relationship between a teacher and a pupil, or between a master and an apprentice. So when you see the word "teacher," it is not just describing one who teaches, but one who has a relationship with those who are being taught. For example, if you regularly watch Rick Renner's program and are learning the truths and principles he teaches each day, you're forming a "teacher-student" relationship with him. Likewise, if you sit and receive godly wisdom from your pastor each week, you are his pupil, and he is your masterful teacher. That is what the word *didaskalos* describes — the relationship between the teacher and the pupil.

We see this relationship clearly demonstrated between Jesus and His disciples. In John 13:13, Jesus told His disciples, "Ye call me Master and Lord: and ye say well; for so I am." The word "Master" here is the Greek word *didaskalos*. By using this word, Jesus was saying, "I have a masterful voice in your lives. I am a masterful Teacher, and because you have sub-mitted to Me as My students and My apprentices, I am also Lord. I have a voice of authority in your lives." The word *didaskalos* doesn't just describe a person who gives information, but one who has a voice of authority to speak into your life. This is very important when you consider the ministry of a New Testament teacher.

History reveals that such teachers would literally sit right alongside their pupils and watch them work and would speak into their ears as they hovered over them. It was the student's responsibility to listen, to obey, to internalize what his teacher said, and then to carry it out in daily life. Thus, the word "teacher" —the Greek word *didaskalos* — inherently has great authority connected to it. So much so that it is most often translated as the word "master" in the New Testament. A "teacher" has a masterful grip on the Scriptures and great authority over his students. All of this meaning is contained in the word "teacher" (*didaskalos*).

Being a Teacher Is a Serious Responsibility

James, the brother of Jesus, made a very sobering statement regarding those who function in the fivefold ministry of a teacher. He said, "My brethren, be not many masters, knowing that we shall receive the greater condemnation" (James 3:1). The word "many" here is the Greek word *polloi*, which describes *a great number*.

The word "masters" in this verse is the Greek word *didaskalos*, and it describes *a teacher, one who is a fabulous, masterful teacher*. It is the Greek equivalent of the Hebrew word for *rabbi*. Again, this is not just a person who stands up and reads Scripture and offers their personal commentary on it. This is a God-anointed, God-appointed individual who has a masterful grip on the entire Word of God.

Through James, the Holy Spirit cautions believers not to aspire to the role of "teacher." Why? He said because they "…shall receive the greater condemnation" (James 3:1). The word "greater" is the Greek word *meidzon*, which means *far greater by comparison*. And the word "condemnation" is the Greek word *krima*, which describes *a verdict or judgment that results from a formal investigation*. The Holy Spirit's use of this word *krima* tells us that those who publicly teach and claim they are a fivefold ministry teacher will be scrutinized by God Himself — He will watch to see if what they endorse or teach is in agreement with the entire body of Scripture. He Himself will investigate and issue a judgment of every fivefold ministry teacher.

This means every word, every phrase, and every nuance that is spoken in a public forum by a spiritual leader is significant to God. This is a powerfully sobering truth. We can see just from the witness of this one scripture why it is so important for Christian leaders to always remember that words have consequences. Truth sets people free, but error enslaves people. This verse specifically says teachers will be judged more strictly and will be held to a higher standard. It is sobering for those of us who teach — for nothing like this is said of apostles, prophets, evangelists, or any other ministry. That speaks of the importance of teachers!

Apostles are given by Christ to the Church to establish churches. *Prophets* are given to the Church to speak on behalf of God. *Evangelists* are given to the Church to channel good news and God's supernatural power, especially to the lost. *Pastors* are given to the Church to shepherd the local congregations. But Jesus gave *teachers* to the Church to set forth truth from God's Word, and that powerful truth has the divine ability to liberate people and to change their lives. If what is being taught is error, it can mess up people's lives terribly. **Truth is the goal!**

A Desire to Be a Teacher Is Not Enough — One Must Be Firmly Established in Truth

The apostle Paul also wrote about teachers — specifically *false teachers*. In First Timothy 1:7 he said, "Desiring to be teachers of the law; understanding neither what they say, nor whereof they affirm." The word "desiring" in this verse is the Greek word *thelo*, which means *to earnestly desire* or *to long for*. It depicts *an earnest or an ongoing desire*. In this case, it is a deep yearning to be "teachers of the law," which is the Greek word *nomodidaskalos*. This is a compound of the word *nomos*, meaning *rules, principles, or the unchanging and unbendable rule of faith*, and the word *didaskalos*, which is the word for *a masterful teacher* that we've been studying. When these two words are compounded to form the word *nomodidaskalos*, it pictures *a masterful scripture-lawyer, someone scholarly in interpreting the Bible*.

So Paul is telling us that some people have an earnest desire to be masterful Scripture-lawyers. The problem, however, is that they "…understanding neither what they say, nor whereof they affirm" (1 Timothy 1:7). The word "understanding" is from the Greek word *noountes*, which is a derivative of the word *nous* — the Greek word for *the mind*. The word *noountes* means *to perceive* and *refers to the mind and the ability to think, reason, understand, and comprehend*. In this verse, it means *not comprehending; to be defective in one's ability to think, reason, and understand*. Even though these aspiring teachers may have partial understanding of Scripture, they are missing many key pieces of the biblical picture. As a result, they are arriving at wrong doctrinal conclusions.

Also notice the word "affirm." Paul said, "…understanding neither what they say, nor whereof they *affirm*" (1 Timothy 1:7). The word "affirm" is the Greek word *diabebaioomai*, and it means *to continuously assert; to continuously establish or affirm confidently*. The Greek text actually says, "They don't understand what they are constantly alleging and reporting." That is, they are trying and trying and trying to prove a point, but it cannot be proven because their conclusion is incorrect.

Paul said that as much as these individuals long to be Scripture-lawyers, they cannot be because they themselves are not established in the truth — they are not equipped to stand in the position of a fivefold ministry teacher. Although they may be called to the position, they are not ready for it yet. A Christ-given teacher must do all he or she can do to understand the Scriptures and be well-versed in them.

A Picture of a Well-Versed Teacher From the Old Testament

A great example of a well-versed teacher from the Old Testament is Ezra. The Bible says, "This Ezra was a scribe, [who] was well versed in the law... (Ezra 7:6, *NLT*). The *New King James Version* of this verse says Ezra "... was a skilled scribe in the law...."

What exactly did Ezra do with the Word of God that was so great? Nehemiah 8:8 (*NIV*) says, "They read from the Book of the Law of God, making it clear and giving the meaning so that the people could understand what was being read." The *New Living Translation* says, "They read from the Book of the Law of God and clearly explained the meaning of what was being read, helping the people understand each passage." Looking at the *New American Standard Bible*, it says, "They read from the book, from the law of God, translating to give the sense so that they understood the reading." And the *New King James Version* says, "So they read distinctly from the book, in the Law of God; and they gave the sense, and helped them to understand the reading."

Ezra knew the people needed to understand the Scriptures. He was speaking to Jews that had been in captivity for 70 years, most of whom did not understand the original Hebrew language in which the Bible was written. In order for him to be able to make the meaning of the Scriptures clear and help the people understand each passage, he had to be a masterful teacher. He had to have had a powerful grip on the Scriptures.

With the reading of each verse, Ezra took time to *translate* and *explain* its original meaning. In the same way, part of the ministry of the New Testament teacher is to *translate* and *explain* the meaning of the

Scriptures. They are to take the original Hebrew and Greek language and communicate the essence of its meaning into the common language so that people can understand.

Like Ezra, the New Testament teacher is a *didaskalos* — he is a *masterful teacher-scholar, a rabbi, one who possesses a great accumulation of facts and knowledge.* The more a Bible teacher knows, the more he or she can be used by the Holy Spirit. Being full of the Word of God, the Spirit can draw out and bring to the surface countless different truths out at any given moment. He or she is a ready vessel. Ultimately, the goal of teacher is to provide teaching people can trust.

STUDY QUESTIONS

Study to shew thyself approved unto God, a workman that needeth not to be ashamed, rightly dividing the word of truth.
— 2 Timothy 2:15

In addition to the fivefold ministry gift of *teacher*, God has also given you an internal Teacher that is always with you — a *Didaskalos* that is All-knowing and never makes mistakes. He is the Holy Spirit! Jesus had a lot to say about the Holy Spirit serving as your Teacher. Check out these verses and make a note of when, where, and what you can call upon Him to teach you.

1. Matthew 10:18-20 and Luke 12:11,12
2. John 14:15-17, 26; 1 John 2:27
3. John 16:7-15
4. 1 Corinthians 2:9-12

PRACTICAL APPLICATION

But be ye doers of the word, and not hearers only, deceiving your own selves.
— James 1:22

1. In what specific ways have you experienced the teaching ministry of the Holy Spirit?
2. What could you tell someone to encourage them to seek out and listen for the teaching and coaching ministry of the Holy Spirit in his or her life?

3. Has the teaching voice of the Holy Spirit grown quiet in your life? Take time to pray and ask God if there's anything you've done to grieve or quench His work in your life (*see* Ephesians 4:29-32; 1 Thessalonians 5:19-22). Repent of anything He reveals that is separating you from His manifest presence, and take any action steps He prompts you to take.

Notes

Notes

Notes

_____

_____

_____

_____

_____

_____

_____

_____

_____

_____

_____

_____

_____

_____

_____

_____

_____

_____

_____

_____

_____

_____

_____

_____

_____

_____

_____

_____

Notes

Notes

Notes

Notes

Notes

Notes

Notes

www.ingramcontent.com/pod-product-compliance
Lightning Source LLC
Chambersburg PA
CBHW060403050426
42449CB00009B/1886